D1288038

THE INQUIRING MIND

The Inquiring Mind

CYRIL O. HOULE

The University of Wisconsin Press

MADISON, 1961

Published by The University of Wisconsin Press,
430 Sterling Court, Madison 6, Wisconsin

Copyright © 1961, by the Regents of the
University of Wisconsin

Printed in the United States of America
Second Printing

Library of Congress Catalog Card No. 61-7496

To Bettie

FOREWORD

The University of Wisconsin-Milwaukee considers it a real privilege to have had on its campus during the spring semester of 1960 as Knapp Visiting Professor, Dr. Cyril O. Houle, Professor of Education, The University of Chicago. Professor Houle is the first holder of this professorship since the University of Wisconsin-Milwaukee became an integral part of the University of Wisconsin and thus became eligible for participation in a program made possible through the generosity of Kemper K. Knapp.

It is significant that Professor Houle, who has distinguished himself in the field of adult education, should have been invited to deliver this first series of lectures in his particular area of specialization. Serving the adult population by providing a wide variety of educational services has been deeply embedded in the University of Wisconsin tradition since the turn of the century when "The Wisconsin Idea" came into being and made available to the people of the State the academic and intellectual resources of the University. More specifically, however, the University of Wisconsin-Milwaukee has committed itself to a working partnership with a community that is richly endowed with a variety of adult education activities, and that because of these resources has long been considered an ideal laboratory for bringing "town and gown" together for the purpose of improving community living.

Dr. Houle's penetration into the inquiring mind, it is hoped, will cause others to carry on investigation in an area where little has thus far been done. Dr. Houle has pioneered in seeking answers to what prompts the adult to want to learn and continue his education after he has completed its formal phase. The ensuing lectures are most suggestive in this regard and future researchers delving into the mysteries of the adult mind should find many avenues of explanation opened up to them by this series of lectures.

J. Martin Klotsche
Provost
University of Wisconsin-Milwaukee

PREFACE

Kemper K. Knapp was born a hundred years ago in Marquette, Wisconsin. In due course he entered and was graduated from the University of Wisconsin, receiving his B.S. in 1879 and his LL.B. in 1882. Though he went immediately to Chicago and practiced law there until his death, sixty-two years later, he retained a deep interest in the welfare of his Alma Mater, and it expressed its own esteem by awarding him an honorary LL.D. in 1930. His bequest to the University was the largest in its history and was notable as well for its breadth of viewpoint. He limited his gift to no condition of use except that it be for the University's benefit.

In memory of Mr. Knapp, the Board of Regents established a visiting professorship which is University-wide in scope. One of the assignments of the Knapp Professor is to deliver a series of public lectures. It was my honor to hold the Professorship on the Milwaukee campus of the University during the spring semester of 1960; this volume contains the lectures given on that occasion.

An audience drawn from many disciplines as well as

from the general public expects that a speaker will deal with a theme of widespread interest. Accordingly I chose a topic which, though it is at the heart of the specialized field of adult education, should also be a matter of concern to everyone: what kinds of men and women retain alert and inquiring minds throughout the years of their maturity? In view of the importance of this question, there have been surprisingly few efforts to answer it and I hoped that the exploratory inquiries reported here would lead to further investigation.

The wish that the lectures would initiate rather than conclude discussion has already been fulfilled to some extent. In the months since the talks were delivered, a number of those who heard them have been good enough to challenge certain points and provide supporting evidence for others. The lectures were delivered from notes in the hope that a direct approach would be more interesting to the audience than a prepared address. In writing down my remarks later on, I have not hesitated to make such changes as were suggested by the deeper insights which discussion with my Wisconsin colleagues provided.

The Social Science Research Committee of The University of Chicago provided a small grant to support the research; further assistance was given by the W. K. Kellogg Foundation. Earl Hargett conducted some of the interviews and helped with most of the others, and his wife assisted us both in making the results of those interviews intelligible. The manuscript has been read and criticized not only by Mr. Hargett but also by Professor Harold Dunkel and by my wife, both of whom made numerous acute observations. Professor James Lea Cate and Miss Marie Beall suggested several historical and biographical sources. Michael Burns labored over the text with me and made many valuable suggestions for changes, both great and small. Lawrence Allen assisted with the bibliographic references. I am grateful to all of them, to J. Martin Klotsche for writing the Introduction, to the two sources of financial support, and to the many other people who have helped clarify the ideas presented here but who cannot be held responsible for the final result.

My debt is particularly great to those who allowed me to interview them and to my friends who helped locate people to be interviewed. I trust that I have justified their confidence in me and only my promise of anonymity keeps me from proudly including the names of all of them. (This anonymity has been further preserved by changing unessential details in describing individuals.)

Most important, I would like to express gratitude to the faculty and administration of the University of Wisconsin-Milwaukee. This second campus of the University is only five years old but it has already attracted national interest by its stimulating new approach to the provision of higher education in a metropolitan community. It has been an honor to be associated, even though briefly, with this effort to preserve and re-interpret in a challenging new setting the traditions of an old and great university.

Cyril O. Houle

July, 1960

CONTENTS

THE INQUIRING MIND

I

TWO EDUCATIONS

Every man who rises above the common level has received two educations: the first from his teachers; the second, more personal and important, from himself.—Edward Gibbon [1]

THE DESIRE to learn, like every other human characteristic, is not shared equally by everyone. To judge from casual observation, most people possess it only fitfully and in modest measure. But in a world which sometimes seems to stress the pleasures of ignorance, some men and women seek the rewards of knowledge—and do so to a marked degree. They read. They create or join groups in order to share their studies. They take courses. They belong to organizations whose aims are wholly or partly educational. They visit museums and exhibits, they listen to radio and watch television with discrimination, and they travel to enlarge their horizons. The desire to learn seems, in fact, to pervade their existence. They approach life with an air of openness and an inquiring mind.

[1] *Autobiography*, Everyman Edition (New York: E. P. Dutton, 1923), p. 66.

No sharp line divides such people from the rest of mankind. Like the beautiful, the gifted, or the intelligent, they possess to a marked degree what all men and women have in some measure. Everyone might be placed somewhere on a single scale ranging from the most avid to learn to the most incurious, if only we knew what kind of progression to set up and how to establish its stages. But even those at the lowest end of any such scale would still have some wish to learn. It would be hard to think of any adult so content with a semi-vegetative routine of eating, working, sleeping, and staring at the basilisk eye of television that he does not sometimes wonder, and act as a result of his wonderment. Even Ortega y Gasset's "mass-man," whose image has so greatly influenced modern sociology, must occasionally learn how to be more like everyone else.

An examination of the learning habits of all mankind must wait for another time and a broader investigation. My purpose here is only to mark off for exploration a small part of that larger inquiry, hoping not so much to cover even that small sector as to uncover its significance so that it may become the subject of later and fuller development. Let us center attention, then, not on all continuing learners but on those adults who engage to an outstanding degree in activities which are commonly thought to be educational. About such people we shall ask the usual questions—who, what, when, where, and why—and examine such other more complicated matters as may seem appropriate.

My words show, and are meant to show, a general bias in favor of the continuation of learning throughout life and an approval of most of those who engage in it. Popular practice does not, it is true, suggest that this view-point is universally, or even widely, shared, but it underlies the pages which follow and should be made explicit. Unlike the natural scientist, who does not necessarily feel any emotional attachment to the protons or paramecia he studies, the social scientist usually finds that his own beliefs are involved in his examination of phenomena. The best he can do is to indicate which way his own sympathies lie and then get on with as rigorous an examination of the data as he can manage, trying to be sure that his conclusions flow from his facts and not from his feelings. Such at any rate is the conviction guiding my own observations.

THE WEALTH of studies dealing with participation in adult education is a clear-cut indication of the importance which other investigators have attached to that subject, perhaps because of the prodigious growth of all organized forms of adult education. Numerous as such studies are, however, they all pursue a single general theme, the effort to discover the characteristics of those people who are served by one or more of the established educational institutions or associations. Who uses the public library? What kinds of people go to the evening school, the evening college, the museum, the community center, the settlement house, or the extension class? Who is reached by the agricultural or home economics programs sponsored by land-grant colleges and other authorities? Who belongs to the clubs, councils, and conferences, the societies and associations, the leagues and lodges which are so widespread in our society? These and similar questions have prompted investigations at many levels of complexity, from simple service studies to sustained pieces of research using rigorous techniques and sophisticated designs.

The findings are fairly consistent and hold few surprises for anyone who is generally knowledgeable about current patterns of social action. Two excellent and readable summaries have recently been completed [2] and may be consulted by those who wish a detailed analysis. In very broad outline, the results lead to the following general conclusions.

To begin with, every adult educational program has usually been developed in terms of more or less explicit conditions which limit its clientele. This point is obvious in the case of the education department of a union, a management training school operated by an industry, or the League of Women Voters. Even in those institutions with ambitions for universal service, such as the public library, the university extension division, or the evening school, the difference between aim and accomplishment is sometimes very great. The people actually served turn out to be drawn chiefly or entirely from the middle class, the relatively highly educated, and the professional or clerical occupations.

While the clientele of each institution has its unique features, certain characteristics are common to all the groups served. In general, high income groups are more

[2] Edmund deS. Brunner and others, *An Overview of Adult Education Research* (Chicago: Adult Education Association, 1959); Coolie Verner and John S. Newberry, Jr., "The Nature of Adult Participation," *Adult Education*, VIII (Summer, 1958), 208–22.

likely to take part in educational activities than low income groups. Participation is also positively related to
the size of the community, the length of residence in it,
and the number of different kinds of educational activity
available. People with certain nationality or religious
backgrounds are more active than those with other backgrounds. Age is important: the very young adult seldom
takes part, but there is a sharp upturn in the late twenties,
a fairly constant level of activity until the age of fifty,
and a decline afterward. Married people participate more
than single people, and families with school-age children
more than families without them. Many more professional, managerial, and technical people take part relative
to their number in the population than do people from
other occupational groups; next in significance are white-
collar and clerical workers; then skilled laborers; and
lastly unskilled laborers. But the most universally important factor is schooling. The higher the formal education of the adult, the more likely it is that he will take
part in continuing education. The amount of schooling
is, in fact, so significant that it underlies or reinforces
many of the other determinants, such as occupation, size
of community, length of stay in it, and nationality and
religious backgrounds.

These factors cannot be treated merely as separate influences. In practice, they are all related to one another,
sometimes in unexpected ways. In cities, for example,
single people are more active participants than married
people, whereas the reverse is true elsewhere. To choose
another illustration, women are more active than men in
church-related groups, but men are more active than
women in secular groups. As the various factors are added

together, the picture grows more and more complicated. Among middle-class people in cities, women attend meetings more frequently than men, but men belong to more organizations. Present research findings make possible the tracing of even more intricate patterns of analysis than the ones illustrated, but these will serve to show how complex the combination of influences may become.

As already noted, these studies usually start with the act of participation in the program of a single institution, often a relatively formal one. While the value of this line of inquiry is suggested both by its results and by the number of investigators who have chosen it, the approach has certain limitations. It deals with single actions of individuals, not with their whole patterns of educational effort. It describes what men do, and not what they think about what they do, or why they do it. It delimits and routinizes the scope of ventures into learning. ("Italy was my University," said Robert Browning,[3] and "a whale-ship was my Yale College and my Harvard," said Ishmael in *Moby Dick*, but none of these studies could have counted them or anyone like them.) Most significantly, such research merely establishes probabilities. It tells us where to look if we want to find most continuing learners; but, as everyone knows, they are also to be found among the poor, among the isolated, among the newcomers to a community, among the old, among the single, among those who do humble labor, and among those with little formal education.

Many of these limitations would be transcended, though others would be imposed, by research which takes

[3] Quoted in William Sharp, *Life of Robert Browning* (London: Walter Scott, 1890), p. 56.

as its starting-point not the act of participation but the participant. We would then not judge men by individual acts, but would judge such acts by the men who perform them. The results, particularly as they complement the findings of the usual line of investigation, might be illuminating. The study of continuing education is impoverished if it is blind to the personal reflections of such men as Descartes, who was intensely conscious of himself as a continuing learner but slipped through all the categories of formal participation: ". . . as soon as my age permitted me to pass from under the control of my instructors, I entirely abandoned the study of letters, and resolved no longer to seek any other science than the knowledge of myself, or of the great book of the world. I spent the remainder of my youth in travelling, in visiting courts and armies, in holding intercourse with men of different dispositions and ranks, in collecting varied experience, in proving myself in the different situations into which fortune threw me, and, above all, in making such reflection on the matter of my experience as to secure my improvement." [4]

The decision to focus the present inquiry on the individual was reinforced by the perplexing fact that no such studies have previously been undertaken, a gap which has been independently noted by other summarizers of the literature.[5] The proper place to begin such an examination would appear to be with the people who

[4] *Discourse on Method* (London: William Blackwood and Sons, 1863), p. 52.

[5] ". . . participation has thus far not been studied from the viewpoint of the participant or potential participant."—Brunner and others, *An Overview*, p. 118.

are most actively engaged. If we are ever to understand the total phenomenon of continuing education, we must begin by understanding the nature, the beliefs, and the actions of those who take part to the highest degree.

As THE EXAMPLES of Browning and Descartes suggest, the continuing learner has existed in every age. To anyone with a classical education, examples from antiquity come readily to mind. Plato's dialogues and the contemporary descriptions of the Lyceum and other schools testify to the passion for lifelong learning among at least a few of the Greeks. The works of Plutarch, Cicero, and the other Roman writers are rich with illustrations; among them are Cato learning Greek at eighty, Alexander carrying the works of Homer with him everywhere, and Caesar trying to plan each day so that it would include administration, sleep, writing, and study. Even in the ages we now call dark, there were men for whom study was a matter of great importance. Witness this description of Charlemagne by his secretary:

He was not satisfied with command of his native language merely, but gave attention to the study of foreign ones. . . . He most zealously cultivated the liberal arts, held those who taught them in great esteem, and conferred great honours upon them. He took lessons in grammar of the deacon Peter of Pisa, at that time an aged man. Another deacon, Albin of Britain, surnamed Alcuin, a man of Saxon extraction, who was the greatest scholar of the day, was his teacher in other branches of learning. The King spent much time and labour with him studying rhetoric, dialectics, and especially astronomy; he learned to reckon, and used to investigate the motions of the heavenly bodies most curiously, with an intelligent scrutiny. He also tried to write, and used to keep tablets and blanks in bed under his pillow, that at leisure hours he might accustom his hand to form the letters; however, as he did not begin his efforts in due season, but late in life, they met with ill success.[6]

Whole cultures have been based on the conception of lifelong learning, and the Renaissance is the archetype of such a culture. The many-sided men of fifteenth-century Italy, whatever their calling in life, felt it necessary to be learned in many things, sometimes in everything. Burckhardt notes of the period that "There is no biography which does not, besides the chief work of its hero, speak of other pursuits all passing beyond the limits of dilettantism" and goes on to say that, among the many-sided men, there were some whose achievements in learning were so great as to make them all-sided.[7] Napoleon, not, to be sure, a Renaissance man, captured its essence when he defined happiness as "the highest possible development of my talents."[8]

We do not need to explore every other age in a tedious search for continuing learners; every era has produced men and women with keenly inquiring minds. It is worthy of note, however, that in the late eighteenth and early nineteenth centuries, when the desire for the spread of education was far outrunning the possibilities for expansion of the existing schools, one commonly sug-

[6] Einhard, *Life of Charlemagne*, translated from the text of the *Monumenta Germaniae* by Samuel Epes Turner (New York: American Book Company, 1880), pp. 61–62.

[7] Jacob Burckhardt, *The Civilization of the Renaissance in Italy* (New York: The Modern Library, 1954), pp. 104–7.

[8] Quoted in Emil Ludwig, *Napoleon* (New York: Liveright Publishing Corporation, 1943), p. 37.

gested solution was "self-education." The word "self-taught" has a respectable number of entries, showing various degrees of approbation, in the Oxford English Dictionary, and those who liked more technical language developed the term "auto-didactics." Of the modest shelf-ful of books on the subject, the most widely quoted at the time was an expansion of a lecture given by William Ellery Channing to a group of working men.[9] The only such volume which approaches the realm of literature is De Quincey's *Letters to a Young Man Whose Education Has Been Neglected*, but a reading of this work suggests that it is still in print not because of its own merit but because of the eminence its author won by the other products of his pen.

W‍HILE HISTORIES and biographies provide a valuable perspective for the study of the continuing learner, they do not permit very much analysis, chiefly because their authors approach the idea of adult education in such different ways. Some historians and biographers ignore it and others give it only such weight and interpretation as seem appropriate in the light of their particular viewpoints. Also, although Carlyle defined history as "the essence of innumerable Biographies," [10] most of those biographies have never been written. Each age provides a record of its famous men, but not of that far larger number of forgotten people whose unchronicled lives help to give form and content to their times.

[9] *Self-Culture* (Boston: James Munroe and Company, 1839).
[10] "On History," *Critical and Miscellaneous Essays* (Boston: Munroe and Company, 1839), p. 247.

My effort in this study, therefore, has been to examine the lives of a group of adults who are members of our own society. These men and women share a common characteristic: they are so conspicuously engaged in various forms of continuing learning that they could be readily identified for me by their personal friends or by the counselors and directors of adult educational institutions. Otherwise they vary widely in age, sex, race, national origin, social status, religion, marital condition, and level of formal education. All of them live in urban areas, though not necessarily in large cities. University faculty members and people working for degrees were excluded since they make up two groups for whom continuing education is a special way of life.

All of these people were asked by someone in whom they had confidence to participate in an interview; when they agreed, they were provided with a statement describing the nature of continuing education and indicating the general kinds of questions which the interviewer would ask. This statement and the interview schedule itself (both of which had been pre-tested by all of the usual means) included nineteen major questions, all of them worded with an effort to avoid bias. These questions were not asked in any established order and, indeed, each person interviewed was encouraged to talk freely and frankly; often, in the course of a single long monologue, he would answer several questions. The interviews were tape-recorded and later transcribed.

Originally it was planned to collect about twenty case studies but the number was increased to twenty-two in order to be sure that variations in all the characteristics mentioned above were included. This group of cases is in no sense to be considered a statistical sample; it is much too small for that, and there is no way to be certain as yet of the dimensions of the total population which should be represented. Occasionally some clusterings of response appeared to be significant; they will be reported at the appropriate places but with no thought that they are typical of all continuing learners.

Preliminary interviews and discussions had revealed that many people have fairly definite ideas about continuing learners, particularly about why they are the way they are. Some observers lay stress on early family influence, others on the inspiration provided by great teachers, and still others on intelligence or other personal characteristics. As for myself, I had no conscious hypotheses. Many hours spent in counseling adults in search of education have made it easy for me to think of countless exceptions to any simple explanation which others might propose. The interviews were so designed, however, as to encourage the exploration of all of the themes suggested in the preparatory discussions. In a sense I was searching for hypotheses in this small group of case studies, each of which was subjected to detailed analysis. More important, I hoped that these people and their activities could somehow be fitted together into patterns that would throw light on the meaning of continuing education.[11]

These lectures present the patterns which were found. Their significance must initially be judged by whether they appear to be reasonable and in accord with other known facts, but I hope that they will eventually be

[11] For further details concerning this investigation, see "A Note on Method," p. 83.

tested, and broadened, by more rigorous and sharply defined investigations.

TAKEN AS A WHOLE, the group of people, however diverse their backgrounds in other ways, did turn out to be basically similar. They are perceived by others as being deeply engaged in learning and this perception proved to be valid, for they themselves regard continuing education as an important part of their lives even though they differ from each other in their ways of considering it. While there were gradations within the group in the amount, the kind, and the purposes of their study, everyone interviewed would be near the upper end of any scale which measured the extent of people's participation in educational activities. Moreover, they had the same basic ways of thinking about the process in which they were engaged. They all had goals which they wished to achieve, they all found the process of learning enjoyable or significant, and they all felt that learning was worthwhile for its own sake.

But while they were basically similar, they did vary in terms of the major conception they held about the purposes and values of continuing education. As I pondered the cases, considering each one as a whole, it gradually became clear (after many an earlier effort at analysis had led nowhere) that within the group there were in essence three subgroups. The first, or, as they will be called, the *goal-oriented*, are those who use education as a means of accomplishing fairly clear-cut objectives. The second, the *activity-oriented*, are those who take part because they find in the circumstances of the learning a meaning which has no necessary connection, and often no connection at all, with the content or the announced purposes of the activity. The third, the *learning-oriented*, seek knowledge for its own sake. These are not pure types; the best way to represent them pictorially would be by three circles which overlap at their edges. But the central emphasis of each subgroup is clearly discernible.

THE GOAL-ORIENTED are the easiest to understand, chiefly because their views accord so well with the usual beliefs about education. "We no more live to know, than we live to eat," said John Ruskin,[12] and most people, if they gave the matter any thought, would agree with him. Knowledge is to be put to use, and, if it is not, why bother to pursue it?

One person who holds such a view is a solid, heavy-set man of fifty, with an air of both substance and vigor. His face is rather pleasantly like that of a bulldog. He started out as an unskilled laborer in the factory of a large corporation, has now risen through several levels of supervisory responsibility, and will almost certainly rise further. He has made his way, he feels, by adult education, earning first a high school diploma and then a Bachelor's degree in commerce by this means. He did not take this credit work merely for the symbols of accomplishment it would provide but because he felt he needed to have "the material that you get in high school and college." He also felt that he lacked self-confidence and therefore he took several courses in public speaking, in

[12] *The Stones of Venice*, Everyman Edition, Vol. III (New York: E. P. Dutton, 1907), p. 46.

order "to learn how to think on my feet." He has "put in for" all of the optional courses in management that his company provides.

But the desire to get ahead on his job has not been the only reason for his interest in continuing education. He and his wife had a problem with one of their children and, on the advice of the school psychologist, they belonged, for a while, to a discussion group made up of parents of children with similar problems. He himself, in his mid-forties, had some of the feelings of tension which are so characteristic of that period and took part in a group therapy course. He was elected to the school board in the small suburban town in which he lives, and it seemed sensible to him to join the state association of school board members, to read its literature, and to take part in its meetings. In this same community, there is enthusiastic support "among all the right people" for a concert series in the high school auditorium and he feels he must attend, partly because he is on the school board. After suffering intense boredom for a while, he "sneaked downtown and took some music appreciation courses," and what used to be a duty is now beginning to seem almost a pleasure.

When he describes other people engaged in continuing education, this man is aware that not all of them view it as he does. But he is chiefly sensitive to and sympathetic with other goal-oriented individuals who, like himself, have clear-cut aims they wish to achieve: "One of my present bosses is a real good example of a desirable kind of self-educating man. He started for our company as a worker when the company was just starting. I think he probably finished high school, but not more than that. I don't know if he even finished high school. He is now the plant superintendent. He has attended many classes at night school. He's done a lot of reading and is really a learned man, now. He speaks very well, he can write very effectively, and he is obviously a very mature, cultivated man. This is the kind of thing you like to see as a result of self-education, and he did it on his own, too, because he did all of this through going to night school classes and reading."

The continuing education of the goal-oriented is in episodes, each of which begins with the realization of a need or the identification of an interest. There is no even, steady, continuous flow to the learning of such people, though it is an ever-recurring characteristic of their lives. Nor do they restrict their activities to any one institution or method of learning. The need or interest appears and they satisfy it by taking a course, or joining a group, or reading a book, or going on a trip. To be sure, the awareness of the need or interest is sometimes aroused because a learning resource becomes available. Fairly often with this group, as with the others, a circular received in the mail will announce a book or an activity, and this event will suddenly crystallize a sense of need which has been only vaguely felt before. But the purpose is always what initiates the educational effort, and the means are selected on the basis of whether or not they will achieve that purpose. For example, a few of the goal-oriented read a great deal, not freely or widely but always along lines of well-defined interests or in connection with courses or organizational work. The following observation is typical: "I do a fair amount of reading related to my work. Now this is in the area of magazines and professional journals. This would include magazines in the field of industrial safety, industrial health, fire protection, and, in addition to that, I do a fair amount of reading in the various areas of business management. I'm a member of the Society for the Advancement of Management."

THE ACTIVITY-ORIENTED take part in learning primarily for reasons unrelated to the purposes or content of the activities in which they engage. Those included in this subgroup have many different kinds of reasons for being continuing learners, only a few of which will be illustrated here.

Loneliness leads many people to education. This viewpoint was expressed in its purest form by one rather intense woman:

I wish you people in adult education would stop selling tuitions and start selling cordiality or something, or sort of give a little. I think the people that come really want that as much as learning. Forget about the learning part. They are going to learn anyway. That's what they are paying their money for. There is so much that is drab in this world. The real joy of participation, that's the only thing that I think is overlooked in adult education, and I think that's what adults want. They may not recognize that that's what they want, but put it to the test and see. I think that's as important as learning. It's that ingredient that you don't buy over the counter. The real joy of participation.

The adult educational institution, like the church, is an open and socially accepted place for meeting people and making friends. It has, as it were, a kind of preventive psychiatric role. In a mass society many individuals feel lost. They have little or no intimate fellowship and they miss the sense of belonging to a small natural group in which they are important and respected. Therefore they go in search of a social milieu, and the adult educational institution is one of the places where they look for it. In those evening schools which register their students by having them go to the classrooms on opening night, one will often find people moving along from door to door, peering in to see what kinds of folk are already assembled, and choosing finally to enter that class which seems to have the most potentially agreeable group, regardless of the purpose, the content, or the method of the course.

Some people are attracted to adult educational activities because they hope to find a husband or wife. Counselors, ministers, advice-to-the-lovelorn columnists, and others have been suggesting to people for some years now that adult educational classes are good places for finding suitable marriage partners. Among the cases studied, there were two such people—one man, one woman!—who turned to adult education for this reason, though others also had it as a more or less conscious secondary purpose. The problem in almost every case which I have witnessed, in this study and in other situations, goes much deeper than a wish to choose or to be chosen. The problem lies fundamentally in an individual's realization that he or she has somehow not made a proper adjustment to the normal patterns of behavior in a heterosexual society. Such an adjustment is never easy and it is sometimes impossible; that is why the quest for a husband or wife may lead to lengthy and intensive participation in educational activities. Sometimes the remedy is sought directly in courses which are essentially group therapy or have the alluring words "psychology" or "psychiatry" in their titles; to some men and women, however, such courses are too embarrassing or threatening, so that they join more innocuous classes in which members of the opposite sex are to be found, hoping to learn how to adjust to them. As one acute woman, who had had many courses at the YMCA, observed: "I think the initials YM entice a lot of women here."

Still others are primarily seeking to escape from a basic personal problem or an unhappy relationship. A wretched marriage, a demanding elderly parent, a job which is routine and distasteful: these and other misfortunes can father the wish to escape for a time into an activity which is positive, which provides a contrast to the rest of life, and which can be readily explained.

Another kind of person who falls within this subgroup would be the man or woman who takes courses simply for the credits themselves or for the diplomas, certificates, or degrees which may eventually be won by piling up the proper number and kinds of credits. Such people care little (often nothing) for the subject-matter itself and, at the end of a term, they may be found in a long line at the bookstore selling back the volumes which they had been required to buy and for which they now feel no further need. Some credit-seekers (I hope most of them) really want to know the content of the courses they take and therefore are goal-oriented; but most teachers who have taught credit courses for adults have found in their classes individuals who indicated, usually politely but always unmistakably, that it was only the activity and what its completion could bring that mattered to them.

A few people are continuing learners because they believe that they are in this way carrying on a tradition of their family or their culture. The late George Apley collected Chinese bronzes (in the process trying to inform himself fully about them) but not because he liked them. "As a matter of fact," he noted, "I think many of my best ones are overdecorated and look inappropriate in the Hillcrest library. I have made this collection out of duty rather than out of predilection, from the conviction that everyone in a certain position owes it to the community to collect something." [13] One man interviewed for this study said of his family, "We are forward-moving people. Growth and progress have always been in my background." Here before my eyes was one of Mr. David Riesman's tradition-directed men, perhaps laying an unusual stress on this part of his heritage because (as the rest of the interview showed) it was the only remnant of his tradition left to him.

Finally, there are some individuals who have been engaged in education so long and to such an extent that it has become an essentially meaningless activity. One of the men interviewed was such a person. For more than twenty-five years, he has taken every course available to him, sometimes gorging himself with as many as five or six at once, in a wholly meaningless profusion, with no pattern, coherence, or apparent effect. His latest job, in a lifetime of casual employment, is as a salesman in a

[13] John P. Marquand, *The Late George Apley* (New York: The Modern Library, 1936), p. 163.

hardware store which specializes in radio and electronic equipment. About this job, he says, "Like in any profession you've got to start little and then as you go up you may want to go into part commercial and part industrial and part—like manufacturing radios and television sets and maybe owning stations and maybe—I know there's one man whose name is Sarnoff who made his appearance as a poor boy just like me and he went to New York and he's a millionaire now. If I had stayed at Hart, Schaffner, and Marx, and that's almost 24 years ago, I might have been somebody now. You know, when a man works steadily for like 22 or 24 years, I might have been a big time executive now. If I live to be 55 or 70 or 80 years old, maybe I'll have something then." To hear such a recital as this is to be reminded of the litany which George recited to Lennie in *Of Mice and Men:* "Guys like us, that work on ranches, are the loneliest guys in the world. They got no family. They don't belong no place. They come to a ranch an' work up a stake, and then they go inta town and blow their stake, and the first thing you know they're . . . on some other ranch. They ain't got nothing to look ahead to. . . . With us it ain't like that. We got a future. . . . Someday—we're gonna get the jack together and we're gonna have a little house and a couple of acres an' a cow and some pigs . . . an' live off the fatta the lan'." [14]

All of the activity-oriented people interviewed in this study were course-takers and group-joiners. They might stay within a single institution or they might go to a number of different places, but it was social contact that

[14] John Steinbeck, *Of Mice and Men* (New York: The Modern Library, 1937), pp. 28–29.

they sought and their selection of any activity was essentially based on the amount and kind of human relationships it would yield. Most of them said—and it was believable—that they did almost no reading. If the number of cases was enlarged, however, we might find that the desire for social contact is not common to all of the activity-oriented. As we have seen, some people escape from solitude into a classroom; there must be others who retreat from busyness into the quiet of the library or the museum.

FOR THE LEARNING-ORIENTED, education might almost be called a constant rather than a continuing activity. This subgroup differs from the other two much more markedly than either of them does from the other. Each particular educational experience of the learning-oriented is an activity with a goal, but the continuity and range of such experiences make the total pattern of participation far more than the sum of its parts. To draw a parallel, a man reading a novel may be inferred to have a purpose in mind for reading it, but if he reads five novels a week, year after year, his habitual behavior as a novel-reader is more notable than the act of reading any individual novel. So it is with the learning-oriented; what they do has a continuity, a flow, and a spread which establish the basic nature of their participation in continuing education. For the most part, they are avid readers and have been since childhood; they join groups and classes and organizations for educational reasons; they select the serious programs on television and radio; when they travel, as one woman put it, they "make a production out of it," being sure to prepare adequately to appreciate what they see; and they choose jobs and make other decisions in life in terms of the potential for growth which they offer.

The fundamental purpose which lies back of all this activity is, quite simply, the desire to know. Juvenal identified *cacoëthes scribendi*, the itch to write. These people have *cacoëthes studendi*, the itch to learn.

Such a man was Alfred, the ninth-century ruler of England, one of those gifted but unfortunate people about whom the impression has somehow been created that the life of each consisted of a single anecdote. Whatever Alfred's faults as a cake-watcher, he was the very model of a learning-oriented man, as his biography by his tutor, Asser, shows. The modern translator of Asser sums up the character of Alfred in this way:

. . . while he is no bookworm, he is fully alive to the importance of training the mind no less than the body; he is profoundly convinced of the value of education both for the ruler and the ruled. Every minute that he can spare is devoted to the improvement of his mind . . . he long sought help and opportunity in vain. His intense desire for learning had been thwarted in his early youth, and as he grew to manhood the peril of the state deprived him of the needed leisure. Even when opportunity was at last granted to him, he had not merely to contend with past neglect but also to create the means which should make intellectual advance a possibility. But he does this and more. His naturally quick intelligence was displayed in all his work, and it enabled him to make good the deficiencies in his education. His indomitable will helped him to overcome all other obstacles, permitting neither the lack of early training, nor the many other cares of his position . . . to deter him from the successful pursuit of his object.[15]

Another such person is a thirty-eight-year-old man who is a skilled laborer in an automobile assembly plant. He is married and has four children. He was born of lower-class parents but now is probably in the lower-middle class. He was not able to finish high school, though he would have liked to do so, because the family did not have enough money to permit him to stay. He is a man of muscular physique, who wears glasses and has a crew cut. His manner is dynamic in the extreme and he is often forcefully, though not unpleasantly, dogmatic about his opinions. Here are the salient facts about him assembled from various parts of the interview:

My relationship with my parents was very close and warm. My father had a third-grade education and my mother an eighth-grade education. My father is open-faced, highly gregarious, extremely interested in other people. A non-intellectual type, who reads a great deal, but reads in terms of newspaper material and this type of analysis, who is highly interested in the world and the problems of the world. My mother is not quite as interested as my father is in all the problems of the world. She is not quite as gregarious as he is. We had a really happy home. I wouldn't say we were really unhappy at the time we were there. I never was unhappy. Everything went along pleasantly and smoothly. You know sometimes economically things weren't so good, but that never disturbed me much. I never went hungry. I always had clothes. Whenever I was sick, I went to the doctor. I would say we managed fairly well.

I don't know why I was always interested in learning. I

[15] Asser, *Life of King Alfred*, translated with introduction and notes by L. C. Jane (London: Chatto and Windus, 1908), p. xliii.

can remember when I was a kid, my sister always commented on it. I used to play with her and the other kids, baseball and everything, and then I said, "I'm tired of it. I want to go home and read." I remember I had some relatives that lived in Detroit, Michigan; one of the greatest pleasures in my life was to go and visit them. They had two boys, my first cousins. I had a wonderful time there. Even there I would go to the library and read. We'd go out and play tennis or go to the school ground and play. We used to have an old drum and I'd roll on the drum like a clown in the circus. But I always managed to read something somewhere.

I started using the library early. Had to roller skate twenty blocks there and back. I remember I had my bed; I'd read at night. I'd have the book under my bed. I was raised right behind the elevated tracks. Sometimes the screech of the trains would wake me up. I'd read until I couldn't fight off sleep any more. Then I'd wake up at dawn and reach under the bed and get the book and read again. I always went everywhere with a book, always, my whole life. When my mother used to ask me to go on errands, go to the grocery store and so forth, I am sure I was brutal. "I'm too busy reading; don't bother me"; and she never pressed the point. She allowed me to read, in other words. I used to come to eat and probably dawdle over my food for an hour but I'd be reading while doing it and she never stopped me from doing it. Of course, since I became married I stopped reading at the table. Wife objects.

Reading is still his major activity and he manages to do an incredible amount of it. He is very active in his union educational program, both organizing courses and taking them himself. He has enrolled in a number of university week-end and vacation courses for union members. He joins and participates in organizations which will add to his knowledge; at present he is most active as a committee member for a local YMCA. He listens to FM radio, chiefly as background to his other activities, but he pays close attention to some of the talks and the dramatic presentations. He is equally discriminating about television and his own choices of programs are scheduled in the family's plans for the week.

He has a fairly normal social pattern, though he recognizes that he is "a character." Some of the other men at work call him an egghead, and his wife wishes he would spend a little more time working on the apartment. He regards himself quite clearly as a continuing learner and feels that he is different from others on that score. "I know a very few people who continually try to go to school. Most of the people I know, although they don't say so, seem to think that the studying you do is for a very specific purpose that you can see, and feel, and touch. That is, if you don't see, and feel, and touch, and feel a dollar come out of it, well you just don't do it. What's the meaning of it?"

His own interests are very different from those of such people. "All my mature life I have attempted to study three general areas of thought. And the reason I pursue these, I would guess, is because I thought they were the most meaningful and to give me insight. They are history, economics, and philosophy. These three areas I have continued to read in rather indiscriminately always. I am always interested in every little facet among these three fields and in other areas only in the sense that they are subsidiary to and feed into these three areas. I am not interested in science as such, except as it contributes to my thinking about the world."

Why is he the way he is? "I don't know. All I can say

is, negatively, there was no one to discourage me and positively I always enjoyed it. The more I fed my appetite, the greater my appetite became." *Cacoëthes studendi.*

THIS CASE MIGHT be a good one with which to conclude, stressing, as it does, a number of values which many members of a university audience (being, for the most part, learning-oriented themselves) would almost certainly like to emphasize. But no one of the three orientations is, after all, innately better than the others, and to bring matters back to a more proper balance it may be well here at the end to re-state a point made at the beginning of the analysis of the interviews. All of the people in the sample are basically similar; they are all continuing learners. They have goals; they enjoy participation; and they like to learn. Their differences are matters of emphasis. Most of them fit clearly into one or another of the three groups but none is completely contained thereby. A few people stand so near the boundary between groups that there might be difference of opinion as to where they should properly be classified, but a longer or more skillfully conducted interview might well have removed the indecision about where each belonged.

This classification does not necessarily hold true for those who participate less extensively than the people studied; long experience in continuing education may be needed to build up firm conceptions about it. Nor can the grouping be extended to educational activities themselves; a particular course, for example, may attract representatives of all three groups, each attending for his own distinctive reason. A class in English composition may appeal to an activity-oriented person because it offers him credit, to a goal-oriented person because he needs to know how to express himself to get ahead on his job, and to a learning-oriented person because he is concerned with making himself more skilled in one of the liberal arts, not for its value in reaching other ends but because it is good in and of itself.

If adult learners really fall into these three groups, this fact will be useful in understanding and guiding adult education. But we must not be rigid in forcing people into such categories, for the aims of education are as broad as the range of human perfectibility permits. Adulthood offers to the average individual fifty years in which to learn how to solve his own problems as well as to explore the wonderfully inexhaustible realms of knowledge. The young exult in the power and precision of their bodies. They love the swift race; the well-played game; the sense of coördinated strength, of smoothness, skill, and alertness; and the rugged capacity to pursue hard effort and withstand severe trials. In adulthood, the mind reaches its peak. The man or woman is far more able than the youth to know, to understand, to explore, to appreciate, to discern subtle relationships, to judge, and to look behind the surface of things to their deeper meaning. The strength of the mind and the strength of the body should both be enjoyed, each in its own proper season, and the denial of the mind is as great a tragedy as the denial of the body. There is so much to know and so little time in which to learn it that not even the longest lifetime is enough.

II

STEP TO THE MUSIC

If a man does not keep pace with his companions, perhaps it is because he hears a different drummer. Let him step to the music which he hears, however measured or far away.
—Henry David Thoreau [1]

THE WAY BY WHICH bats navigate in the dark was not finally understood until 1938. Curious-minded people had been speculating about it for centuries, because, while a bat is neither accomplished nor versatile, and is certainly not attractive, it does one thing supremely well. It flies swiftly and unerringly in utter darkness, never bruising itself on obstructions, avoiding the delicate threads which investigators string up to catch it, and finding and devouring tiny insects—all with no benefit of light. For a century and a half, it has been known that the bat accomplished these results by some special acuteness of hearing, for when its ears were blocked it was helpless. But in 1938, Griffin and Galambos at Harvard

[1] *Walden* (Mount Vernon, N.Y.: Peter Pauper Press, undated), p. 311.

University showed that they could destroy a bat's effectiveness equally well by covering its mouth. The bat, it was realized, pilots itself by responding to the reverberations of its own voice.[2]

Sometimes it almost seems that we who try to educate adults or analyze popular culture have, like the bats, been guiding our courses of action chiefly by what comes back to us as echoes from what we ourselves say. True, we have won a certain measure of success—but so have the bats! We are also more complex. Being human, we do not simply emit automatic signals. We note a few facts, we make a judgment, we voice it, and then we respond to the echoes of it. Our response is conditioned by the quality of the sound which returns. E. M. Forster has observed that "There are some exquisite echoes in India; there is the whisper round the dome at Bijapur; there are the long, solid sentences that voyage through the air at Mandu, and return unbroken to their creator. The echo in a Marabar cave is not like these, it is entirely devoid of distinction. Whatever is said, the same monotonous noise replies, and quivers up and down the wall until it is absorbed into the roof. . . . Hope, politeness, the blowing of a nose, the squeak of a boot, all produce 'boum.' "[3] It is not solely in India that the only echo is "boum."

IF WE ARE sufficiently unanimous and vocal, the outside world almost appears to try to behave the way we have

[2] Donald R. Griffin, *Echoes of Bats and Men* (Garden City: Doubleday and Company, 1959), p. 29.
[3] *A Passage to India* (New York: Harcourt, Brace and Company, 1924), p. 147.

announced it should. To take one example, not necessarily the most important, consider the widely noted fact
that enrollment in formal courses of adult education is
heavily vocational. We observe this phenomenon, we
add to it the general idea that the United States is a commercial and industrial society with strongly materialistic
values, and we draw the conclusion that people enroll
in vocational courses because they want to make more
money. If we hope to expand our influence, we then
build up more vocational programs and emphasize the
dollar motive; and thus we further enhance the emphasis
on vocationalism and help people become convinced that
what we offer must be right. If, on the other hand, we
are not vocationally oriented, we decry the crassness of
American society and scold people for it; and thus we do
nothing to make ourselves and our programs more attractive and, on the whole, merely reinforce the value
of vocationalism and the belief that the dollar-making
motive is the true guiding principle of education.

We have been so successful in making our voices re-
verberate in this way that we can reliably count on most
adults to say what we expect to hear. If we ask people
why they come to an adult educational institution—usually setting up the categories on the questionnaire ourselves—we discover that the major reason they come is
to get ahead on the job. In counseling interviews they
ask for "something that will help me in my work" and
may even ask the adviser to conspire with them to find
vocational motives for obviously non-vocational courses.
English literature is taken "so I can learn to express myself better." Art appreciation is valuable because "some
of the higher-ups in the company are interested in art."

Registration in a course on the fundamentals of science is clearly practical because "we do a lot of technical work and I'd like to know some of the background." Now anybody who knows anything about these three subjects as they are commonly taught is aware that they will not, in any appreciable measure, reach the goals identified and that the prospective students are merely trying, in T. S. Eliot's words, "To prepare a face to meet the faces that you meet." [4] But we go along with the reasoning and accept the motive and sigh that we can do nothing about either, never realizing that in some measure they are but a reverberation of what we as a group have said.

What if the basic idea itself is only partially true? What if reasons other than the desire for occupational success lead people to take vocational courses? Such an idea seems hardly logical, but the experiments by Spallanzani in 1799 which proved that bats navigated by hearing were also ridiculed and rejected until modern physics could detect sounds that lie outside the frequency range of human hearing. The history of scientific investigation is littered with the wreckage of ideas that once seemed wholly logical. Perhaps it is time to cease building up conceptions out of our personal observations of adult learners and discover instead their own self-conceptions.

How do they view themselves and how do they think their associates view them? One way to begin to answer this complex question is to return to an analysis of the three subgroups which have already been identified.

[4] "The Love Song of J. Alfred Prufrock," *Collected Poems, 1909–1935* (New York: Harcourt, Brace and Company, 1936), p. 12.

These three are defined by the conceptions of the continuing learners themselves, but, as we shall see, there are variations of viewpoint within two of them.

THE GOAL-ORIENTED are all alike in their confident acceptance of adult education as a way to solve problems or to pursue particular interests. They describe themselves as seekers after goals, they attribute similar motives to other learners, and the history of their continuing education shows clearly that they have always taken courses or engaged in other forms of activity chiefly because they will be helped thereby. A supervisor in the postal service makes the point very well: "If you made it your business to interview somebody who works in the post office you'd find out that all they can talk about is post office because that is all they know and they really take the post office home with them. The range of the clerks is just the length and width of the building that they work in. Well, now, no matter how rough a day I have at work, I can leave there pretty tired but I can come down here to the University and it does something for me. I attribute to the time I spent in receiving some adult education down here the fact that I have received promotions. If I hadn't had the knowledge I received here through adult education I couldn't have done it."

The goal-oriented are indifferent to and even impatient with any kind of education which is not explainable in their own terms. They seem aware of their penchant for the immediately practical. One industrial chemist, for example, is deeply interested in the issues of the day. He wants to understand the nature of political developments and feel that his voice has influence. At one time he belonged to a discussion group which was largely built around the interests of some learning-oriented men. He explains why he left this group: "I felt this way, that most of their interest seemed to be in classical things, things that happened hundreds, or even a thousand or two thousand years ago, which I know, of course, is related to our present day, but their interests seemed more purely cultural than something which would help us. I was more interested in present-day things, political, foreign affairs, and what not, and they were far more interested in what Julius Caesar did or said."

These people also express more frequently than other groups the desire to keep their minds active. As one poised, self-possessed, fifty-two-year-old professional secretary put it: "Today one must keep on learning to keep on your toes. I don't think it's healthy not to be learning something." At first sight, this appears to be a remark which a learning-oriented person would be most likely to make, but usually he is too busy learning—and therefore keeping his mind active—to think about the need for doing so. The activity-oriented occasionally express this view but not very urgently, and one has almost the sense that they are parroting a viewpoint which they have been told they should have.

As to the activity-oriented, some of them face frankly the fact that they are engaged in continuing education for some reason other than the knowledge it provides. If the reason is socially acceptable, they may even be proud of it, as was the tradition-directed man who felt that study was a part of his heritage. Some of them have enough perspective to deal directly with matters which others conceal, perhaps even from themselves. One woman, for example, was perfectly willing to say that classes are her only social outlet, and one man said that he took part in courses and organizational work because in them he could enjoy a success which eluded him in his occupation.

For the most part, however, when asked directly about their motives, the activity-oriented prefer to say things which, taken at face value, would put them in one of the other categories or even, as with one woman, both: "I take courses partly out of a desire to know and partly out of a feeling that the knowledge might be helpful for living." Only a reading of the entire interview creates the belief that such people are really activity-oriented.

It would, of course, be batlike to suggest that my placement of these people was infallibly correct. In making a decision on this point, heavy reliance was placed on the answers to another question. It was phrased as follows: "As you observe other people who keep on learning, why do you think they do so?" Here, without exception, the people thought to be activity-oriented ascribed motives of this sort to other continuing learners, though not necessarily the same ones which seemed to prompt their own educational efforts. A middle-aged woman for whom education was chiefly an escape from a difficult situation at home and a sterile, superficial social life provided a good illustration of this point. When asked the above question, she answered: "They want to be with people, but not necessarily to develop friendships. You mix with them, you talk with them, and you find out little things that are very indicative. They don't want to participate. They are not capable of giving of themselves and friendship requires a giving, and that's what I mean. They don't have understanding and the joy of listening to others. So they come here where they can be with people on a nice safe basis."

AMONG THE LEARNING-ORIENTED, there are two distinct self-conceptions. Most of the people in this subgroup have long been aware of their own preoccupation with learning (they can cite illustrations from their childhood to prove it), and they recognize that they are different from most other people in this respect. But a few of the learning-oriented insist that they are not continuing learners at all and that education is merely their way of having fun.

Those who believed themselves to be learning-oriented (though they did not use the term itself) had a clarity of self-conception which was evident throughout their interviews, and often they used language which implied an urgent sense of their own difference. When one woman was asked why she thought she was a continuing learner, she said, with an intensity which one would have to hear to appreciate: "I don't know. I'm driven. I don't know. I'm driven." Usually this feeling goes back to childhood. One extremely distinguished man observed, "I had a love of reading very early in life. I don't know where that came from but I'm very thankful to whatever produced it. But I read voraciously and hungrily everything I could get my hands on. Nobody at home did any reading, so there was no reading material at home at all. I wish I could say I read Bunyan's *Pilgrim's Progress* and the Bible, as Lincoln did, but I didn't. But I went through the library and all my high school life I worked in the library as a page. The librarian was very nice to me. Before I finished as a youngster she was letting me read the new books as they came in."

The desire for learning may be so strong that it takes on an almost religious meaning for the individual concerned. Among the people interviewed was a sixty-year-old Negro woman who had been abandoned by her parents at birth, had never had any advantages or very much formal schooling, and had had an incredibly hard existence. And yet, no matter what, she had been drawn to knowledge all her life: "When Billy was a baby in his carriage I used to take him out. I used to go up to the University that's built up on a knoll and right in the back of this knoll there is the hall where the lectures are held. Well, I used to sit in there and listen to all those lectures. I would sit there and even when he got to be three or four years old I still went up there but I taught him that he must be very quiet. He could take his toys or he could take a book, but he must be very quiet. We were never molested; we were never told not to come there." The hero of Thomas Hardy's *Jude the Obscure* moving unseen among the debonair young men of Christminster could not have wanted learning more than this woman did. There was more than a touch of Jude in the fervency with which she described how, after a serious operation and a long illness, she went to a meeting at the suggestion of a friend and, while there, picked up an announcement of a certain adult educational program: "If it had been a gold nugget with a price tag on it I would have taken it! I was just that low in spirits and wanted something to hold onto. So I got it. I took it home with me and I wasn't sure that I was supposed to take it or not but I did. I'd wake up, I'd go to sleep again, I'd wake up and turn the light on and read that book, and I said to my friend, 'You know I've got something here that I can learn. I've got something here, I've got a class here that I can go to.' "

The second self-conception of the learning-oriented —that fun was the sole motive for their educational activity—was held no less firmly than the first. One businessman said, "All I'm seeking is entertainment. It just happens that I get as much fun out of discovering other people's opinions about a picture and arriving at standards for examining pictures or music or literature as maybe some other guy might get out of playing golf. And maybe one reason for that is that I am physically lazy and therefore seek sitting-down entertainment. In other words I'm saying that I'm not so sure that my objective here is to become a richer or broader human being."

Another person with similar views is a forty-year-old branch librarian whose life is so oriented to learning that she provides an excellent illustration of how hard it is to draw the line between education and the rest of life. She has managed to travel widely by taking jobs in a number of places. To hear her tell it, everything she has done has been for fun:

Where does education begin and fun stop? In Cleveland I was doing a lot of reading, more or less under the direction of the staff there. It would be silly to say I did it because they made me, because I enjoyed it. Also I went to ballets for the first time in my life. Is that education or is it pleasure? I went with a girl who helped me understand it, grasp some of its aspects. Then in Seattle, I joined a Great Books program. I did the same in Kankakee. I joined a chess club in Kankakee. Is that education or fun? I can't play chess but it was amusement; it was something one could do in Kankakee!

In Manchester I headed down for London as quickly as I could and managed several week-ends there going to the museums. Well, that's education. Wandering up and down the streets, is that education? Or is it fun? And a week in Wales just looking at things, mostly people. A week in France doing the same sort of thing. Always, I think, if there's a museum or art gallery I can find I go there because I enjoy them. And I suppose, well, obviously, I learn something in the process. I didn't go to any classes—Oh, yes, I did! I went to a class on modern American literature while I was in Manchester. I thought that would be fun hearing an Englishman in England discuss modern American literature. I met some very interesting people and had some wonderful discussions—but at this point I can't tell you what I discussed. I suppose it might be somewhere kicking around in my subconscious. I went out several times with some bird-watchers, but I suppose I saw more pubs than birds.

AND SO WE SEE an involved pattern of self-perceptions, one that is built on the division into three categories but is more complex and diversified. When the question shifts, however, and continuing learners are asked how they think society views them, all three subgroups share clear-cut views of a rather striking sort, and their ideas lead to interesting speculations about the nature—and the future—of adult education in American society.

Let us start with the closest human relationship, marriage. More than half of the people studied were married at the time of the interview. Several had husbands or wives who were also continuing learners, although, in all such cases, they were pursuing patterns of study different from those of the persons interviewed, a fact which might dismay those who exalt the values of togetherness. But one could not but admire the wholesomeness of the relationship between two people who go their separate ways and then share their knowledge with one another. As one man pointed out, "We have a lot of notes that we compare. In other words when we sit down to the table much of our discussion is not so much a discussion of mutual experience as a process of relating to each other our experiences in different directions."

Even where the marriage partner was not a continuing learner, he or she usually supported—or, at least, did not object to—the educational activities of the person interviewed. Here is one example: "My wife is very helpful. She doesn't criticize and I know this is not the case with some men. I know that their wives are critical of an evening away from home or the hours spent in reading. She's become as used to my doing it as I have. She realizes that I'm going to spend at least one evening a week in some kind of educational program and it has become as much a habit with her as it has with me."

Only one person met outright opposition; her husband clearly disapproves of her learning activity. But the evidence throughout the interview was that this whole marital relationship was completely unsatisfactory. The woman remained silent or changed the subject whenever it touched in any way on her husband, and it was obvious that she was pursuing further education despite severe criticism.

Perhaps there is nothing unusual about this almost perfect record of domestic harmony. It may be that husbands and wives generally support one another's activities to the degree indicated here. My own interpretation is different. I believe that, no matter how intensely an individual may want to learn, he or she usually does not do so very actively if the marriage partner objects. The cost of participation on such terms is too great a price to pay.

This conclusion is supported by a small unpublished study by Mr. Edward Weiss, who examined, by motivation research techniques, how middle-class urban men and women felt about the possible participation of their husbands or wives in evening classes. In general the results showed that such people have strong objections to their spouses' taking part in any such activity, believing it to be an effort to escape from home and marital responsibilities.

Pursuing this matter even further, beyond the boundaries of the home, the present study raised the question, "Do people react to the fact that you are a continuing learner?" To try to be sure that the response was valid the question was rephrased in a number of different ways and repeated throughout the interviews, almost always with the same result. The answers were interesting. A few of the respondents claimed they had never thought about the matter, and seemed indifferent to what people might think about their educational efforts. A few said that everybody they knew thought that continuing education was a good idea and that it received their friends' warm approval. But about two-thirds of the total group felt that some or all of their associates were critical of them.

Let us examine this third and largest group. It seems at first sight extraordinary that so many of the people interviewed felt that their friends and associates displayed anything but approval for continuing education. But they put the matter so pungently that it was impossible not to believe them:

"They call me the professor or Einstein or something like that."

"They think I'm a maverick."

"They think I'm creepy."

"They say, 'Aren't you ever going to grow up?'"

"They think I'm crazy."

"The men at work are distrustful of me."

We cannot tell from the interviews whether these people are actually being criticized and scorned as much as they think they are. Perhaps it should be noted that the man who said he was distrusted by the men at work is the president of his local union and the man who said he was considered a maverick had been chairman of the Republican County Committee. But there is no doubt that most of the people studied felt that their learning activities were disparaged by their associates, and often this feeling was intense. The man who was most deeply troubled was a financially successful fifty-year-old merchant who had finally been led by his interest in learning to break with his acquaintances of many years.

I'm not a social person. For years I've been going to dinner parties, one of them more elaborate than the others. And you come in there. There are fifty people and you've got to go up to the bar and take three or four drinks before you begin to feel like moving around at all, and I see fifty people, all of whom I know. You take your drinks, you eat your hors d'oeuvres, you have a fine dinner, and just about the time you are enjoying your dessert, somebody says the card games are about to start. Well, you sit down with three people. Any conversation is taboo. You sit down and you play cards. If you hear a funny remark or if something occurs to you and you say it, well, you're squabbled at, and so forth. I know some of the leading businessmen and lawyers in this town and all I know about them is that they either bid a strong no trump or a weak no trump. And I have been putting up with that for years until this year. This year I just said to heck with them. I don't go to them anymore. It just isn't my kettle of fish. It's caused a lot of comment.

With few exceptions, the people studied here would not regard themselves as "intellectuals," whatever that means, nor would anybody else be likely to classify them in this fashion. If they belonged to a separate group of people distinguished by refinement of taste or devotion to learning, they would be part of a conscious minority which would not expect to be understood or appreciated and which might indeed take a certain satisfaction in its separateness. For the most part, however, they are not distinguished in this way. They have merely taken seriously the widely expressed belief that American society supports education, culture, or self-improvement wherever it is found—and they think they have discovered this belief to be untrue.

Their realization may help to explain the heavy enrollment in vocational subjects which has already been noted. The major reason for this phenomenon is probably the one which is usually given; such courses aid in economic advancement. But in the facts just revealed, there is evidence of a second important reason; a course which seems to shore up or amplify one's money-making power is far easier to justify than one which does not. The wife or the fellows at work may not raise their eyebrows at a course in blueprint reading or commercial arithmetic, or even, if you explain very carefully, at a course in English literature, art appreciation, or the fundamentals of science. But what would they say if you took a course in world politics or modern poetry or Plato? The answer is clear; they might call you the professor, Einstein, a maverick, or creepy, and they would be distrustful of you, perhaps asking, "Aren't you ever going to grow up?"

Those who would like to encourage the growth of continuing education must apparently face the fact that many of the attitudes and values of American society are directly and specifically opposed to the idea of lifelong learning and that this opposition has a vehemence and spread of impact which is not apparent to those who do not feel it directly themselves. The enemy is not apathy, as many would like to believe, but outright opposition, and opposition from places where it counts most—from the family, associates, and friends who surround the person who feels an inclination toward learning.

FOUR OF THE PEOPLE interviewed said that their continuing education was approved by those with whom they were associated. All four lived in a social circle in which the value of study was accepted as natural and fostered as valuable. One is an editor in a publishing firm, where "all of us are the kind of people who are forever taking courses. Of course, my great-aunt up in Dubuque thinks it's very odd!" One is a librarian, all of whose close friends are also librarians. One has built up a congenial circle of friends (and incidentally found a wife) in his various educational activities. One is in a highly creative job in advertising in which he is surrounded by people who value the quest for original thought. Also he lives in a separate section of a high-status suburb where everybody is interested in learning. "We are," he says, "a community of craftsmen."

One of the autonomous or indifferent people also lived in what might be guessed to be a similarly supportive circle, but none of those who reported opposition or criticism were so fortunate.

Apparently our society contains enclaves of people who support continuing education. One man saw this point clearly: "Even though the larger culture in our country doesn't place too great a premium on education but rather on specific achievements, within the larger environment there is a multitude of smaller environments. And I would say that the particular environment within my family which looked with approval on education and which thought reading was purposeful had a great deal to do with my arriving at this mode of existence." The word "enclave" to describe such a "particular environment" is appropriate; the Oxford English Dictionary defines the term as "a portion of territory entirely surrounded by foreign dominions."

The major enclave which supports continuing education for its members is the college or university community. For those whose life is devoted to teaching, truth must be the eternal quest. In the neighborhoods of most such institutions are to be found people who have chosen to settle there because they want to take part in intellectual life and to be with others who think it normal for the mind to be exercised. Other enclaves are found here and there: in certain *avant-garde* sections of large cities, in some parts of exurbia, and, more generally, wherever personal leadership or spontaneous generation has created a social milieu which supports the life of the mind.

These enclaves sometimes take on definite form and structure built around the idea of continuing learning itself, and such organized groups had been influential in the lives of many of the people interviewed. History is full of examples of the self-directing study club or the literary and philosophical society; perhaps the most familiar example is that described by Benjamin Franklin:

. . . in the autumn of the preceding year, I had formed most of my ingenious acquaintance into a club of mutual improvement, which we called the JUNTO. We met on Friday evenings. The rules that I drew up required that every member, in his turn, should produce one or more queries on any point of Morals, Politics, or Natural Philosophy, to be discussed by the company; and once in three months produce and read an essay of his own writing, on any subject he pleased. Our debates were to be under the direction of a president, and to be conducted in the sincere spirit of inquiry after truth, without fondness for dispute, or desire of victory; and, to prevent warmth, all expressions of positiveness in opinions, or direct contradiction, were after some time made contraband, and prohibited under small pecuniary penalties.[5]

[5] *Autobiography* (Boston: Houghton, Mifflin and Company, 1896), pp. 80–81.

The Junto lasted for at least forty years. It has many modern counterparts, some of which have continued even longer than it did.

An informal organization sometimes holds an enclave together very effectively. One was formed some years ago in what might seem an unlikely setting, a naval base in the South Pacific. The young man who reported on it had referred to "a bunch of the fellows" who got together to talk. When asked whether it was "a bunch" or an organized group, he said:

Well, it was the same bunch all the time and I wouldn't say that we said, "Well, at seven o'clock tonight we're going to get together and discuss this problem," but we seemed to be always working on the same sorts of things or wondering about them. And also wondering why we were the only ones that were interested in all this stuff and nobody else. We went into each other's background trying to see what made us so curious about these things that nobody else even cared about. But there didn't seem to be any similarity in the backgrounds that we could find other than we were interested in why we were here in the world and what we were supposed to do and what it all meant. Maybe some of us felt lost and knew that if we could build a philosophy, we'd have security. But some people, I'm sure, didn't feel a need for this, even though I'm sure they didn't have any well-developed philosophy. Maybe the question had never been asked so they didn't feel that they had to answer it.

Some of the fellows came from other huts which was quite an effort if the heat was enough. We made special trips down to the library to gather material to read. My closest buddy happened to work a different shift than I did, so he would read a book, put his marker in, put the book under my mattress; he'd go to work, I'd come and get the book out of the mattress and then later on we'd talk about it.

The other fellows thought we were nuts. I mean, why worry about all these things.

Many of the people interviewed spoke of an event which seemed to each of them remarkable and unique but which, with repetition, came to seem a fairly common phenomenon to me. It was the creation of an enclave by people who were attending the same class. The tone of pride, pleasure, and wonderment in the following passage reflects the general reaction to such an occurrence:

That first class happened to be just a terrific group of people. I've taken other similar things since but I have never hit one where I found such a remarkable group of people. Only about fifteen or twenty, you know, if that many. Most of them were people whom I had never met before, though they lived in the community, and I formed some very good friends during that period. We had a habit after class, a bunch of us, of going over to a little restaurant nearby and having a soda and chatting and as a result of that I got to know a half dozen people who are today my very best friends. And their interests, as you would gather from the fact that they were there, were in that direction, so I would begin to hear about things that I hadn't even considered or wasn't aware of, different kinds of activity, and I would get involved in this or that, not for social reasons but primarily because these people would communicate what they knew about these things and so I belonged.

Some perceptive administrators of adult education have realized the value of providing social support for learning and have tried to turn whole institutions into enclaves. This practice appears particularly congenial to community-centered organizations such as settlement houses, YMCA's, YWCA's, community centers, local

evening schools, and churches and religious groups
which sponsor educational programs. In such settings,
particularly if the building is inviting and conveniently
arranged, a strong spirit of positive morale can be built
up, fostered by effective counseling, social groups and
activities, a staff which is skilled in drawing out and
handling people, and an encompassing student organization. Several of the people interviewed had attended an
institution which is notable for the morale-building features of its program. It was remarkable to see how warmly
they felt about the encouragement the institution gave
them and how much their studies were enhanced by the
social setting. "God bless this place," said one of them,
"it means more to me than anything else."

But enclaves built out of classes and institutions tend
to provide only a temporary and, in some ways, artifi-
cial support for the individual. They seldom gird his life
so intimately or guide it so subtly as family, fellow workers, neighbors, and friends do. If these dominions are
foreign, and there is no other enclave to support the individual, he must carry on his learning against a social
pressure which he will eventually not be able to withstand.

The result is sad enough for those who have never been
awakened to learning, but the tragedy is even deeper
for those who in youth had a zest for knowledge which
they have allowed the cares of maturity to extinguish.
While continuing learners have usually had an extensive
formal education in childhood, not all of those who
have had such an education go on to learn throughout
life. No sensitive teacher of young people can fail to
observe what Irwin Edman calls "the death-in-life that

assails the spirits of young men who had been alive when I knew them in college"; and he adds, "There are times when, if one thought about former students too much, one could not go on teaching." [6] And H. G. Wells considered as "universally tragic" the "incessantly recurring story of high hopes and a grey ending; the story of boys and girls, clean and sweet-minded, growing up into life, and of the victory of world inertia, of custom drift and the tarnishing years." [7]

THOSE WHO TRY to educate adults or who study the best methods of teaching the mature mind are themselves often oriented primarily toward goals, or activity, or learning for its own sake. An educator of adults may maintain that learning always begins with a definition of a need or interest which gives rise to a goal, which then prescribes not only the learning processes but also the method of measuring results. Or he may hold that there is no distinction between educational ends and means, that the engagement of emotion is more important than the imparting of content, and that the non-rational outcomes of learning are more important than the rational ones. (Goethe said about Winckelmann, "We learn nothing by reading him, but we *become* something." [8]) Or the educator of adults may believe that to learn is

[6] *Philosopher's Holiday* (New York: The Viking Press, 1938), pp. 122–23.
[7] *Joan and Peter* (New York: The Macmillan Company, 1926), p. 279.
[8] *Conversations of Goethe with Eckermann and Soret*, translated by John Oxenford (London: George Bell and Sons, 1874), p. 221.

itself a worthwhile pursuit requiring no other justification. A liberal education is necessary, said Sir Richard Livingstone, "not because a sound body, mind and character help to success, or even because they help to happiness, but because they are good things in themselves, and because what is good is worth while, simply because it is good." [9]

Each of these three views is sound but not sufficient, since it cannot comprehend the guiding conceptions of all who seek to learn. Anyone who believes all adult education can be fitted into a single neat pattern is either hearing only the reverberations of his ideas or clinging to the uniformities of a day which is now past. As a field of study matures, it progresses from simple to sophisticated viewpoints, from the certainty of originally perceived truths toward the wisdom which arises from an awareness of complicated patterns, of differences of viewpoint, and of a need to strike a balance among many factors, some conflicting. Both the theory and the practice of adult education are now moving toward this kind of complexity. The simplicities of an earlier era are no longer sufficient either to explain or to guide the growing field. It is no longer possible to assume that the seekers for education will all have consistent viewpoints or that their conceptions will agree with those of the providers of education. The practical consequences of this greater complexity differ from one situation to another, having one kind of significance for a public library, another for an evening college, and a third for a settlement house. But since adult education is voluntary and since the will

[9] "The Future in Education," *On Education* (New York: The Macmillan Company, 1945), pp. 69–70.

to study flows from the self-conceptions of the students themselves, the ideas they express have universal relevance, even though they must be used differently in different situations.

What all those who believe in adult education must do, in common, is to change the set of our society against continuing education. This result may in time be achieved simply by the expansion of activities so that finally, when enough people are involved, intellectual activities will become respectable. The present rate of growth, however, gives little hope that this happy state of affairs will soon be achieved, or that, if it is, the level of socially acceptable activity will be very high. What is needed is a more concerted effort, by educators and such allies as they can enlist among the value-establishers of our society, to express the importance of continuing education as clearly and as universally as they can so that the message finally penetrates to all those different clusters and groups of people who make up the public. Churchill and Eisenhower have made the Sunday painter respectable, and some comparable methods must be found to give social sanction to all those who wish to learn.

But while dramatic national effort is important, anybody who cares to do so can help by trying to establish or to enlarge an enclave made up of those who support the idea that learning is a natural way of life. Perhaps some day the edges of the expanding enclaves will all meet and there will no longer be any surrounding foreign dominions.

III

A CATARACT
OF CONSEQUENCES

*Most medical scientists seem completely oblivious (or ignorant)
of the fact that results usually come from many causes, not
one. . . . We ought to use the word "why" in the plural and
ask, "Whys is this patient in coma?" not, "Why is this patient
in coma?" . . . A particular case of a fractured jaw in a sailor
may be the result of convergent causes—no letters from home,
too much alcohol, the loan of a car by a friend, a dark night,
an oncoming car on a road covered with ice at a curve, the fact
that the left-hand rule is used in the British Isles, new brake
linings, a skid, and a telephone pole. These constitute the whys,
not the why, of a fractured jaw. It is a cataract of consequences.*
                                            —Alan Gregg [1]

OF ALL THE QUESTIONS that can be asked about continuing learners, the most important is "Whys?" There is
no dearth of answers. Almost everyone with whom I
have discussed the subject of these lectures has instantly
favored me with his views on why some people have in-

[1] Alan Gregg, *For Future Doctors* (Chicago: The University
of Chicago Press, 1957), p. 81.

quiring minds and some do not. If everyone agreed, or even if there were majority opinion, the matter might be considered settled; but the viewpoints are many, they are contradictory, and they often reveal more about the people who express them than they do about the subject. Nor can the research already completed offer much greater certainty. But while the answer to "Whys?" is elusive, the continuing learners in this study offer some clues which can be explored by considering two lesser but related questions. Why do such people think they are the way they are? Do their lives fall into any patterns which suggest cause and effect?

ONE INTERESTING FACT about the goal-oriented is that they did not make any real start on their continuing education until after their middle twenties and sometimes not until long after. Before that time, they showed little concern with study; they may indeed have rejected it. Once they had passed the early years of adulthood, however, some crucial incident occurred in the life of each. The foreman called one of them aside and told him he would never amount to anything if he did not get more education. A promotion to supervisor placed another man in a new relationship to all his old associates, and he felt that he would not succeed in his new assignment unless he learned something about administration. Occasionally the crucial incident seemed trivial and born of impulse; one secretary started on a lifetime of study when she and three of her friends decided it would be fun to learn duplicate bridge. In each of these cases, and in all the others like them, three elements came together:

the recognition of a need or an interest, the will to do something about it, and the opportunity to do so.

More important than the external event is the internal process which makes the event, when it occurs, crucial in changing the pattern of life. One is reminded of how, in the classic accounts of religious conversion, the final event which caused belief—the reading of a particular passage in the Bible or the flowering of a pear tree—was foreshadowed by a series of occurrences whose significance it alone could make evident. The young man whom the foreman called aside had probably had many another similar piece of advice in the eight years since he quit school on his sixteenth birthday, vowing that learning was not for him. Why did he listen now? Was it only that he was older and therefore had more perspective? If this were true, then all those in similar circumstances would start to learn in their mid-twenties, and it is clear that they do not. It is more likely that this young man was different from others because he had experienced a series of changes within himself, had observed what happened to other people, and had subconsciously revised his own values. The words of the foreman had meaning for him, whereas those same words uttered to others who have not experienced such inner changes have no effect.

One young woman who had been reared in a stifling, restrictive, self-sufficient family was almost thirty before she began to break out of the hard shell in which her personality had been encased. "What actually made me start," she said, "was the wedding of my friends. In my church, which is quite a narrow-minded group, dancing is strictly forbidden. I had sort of resented going to a lot of my friends' weddings and not being able to join in with the festivities like other people did, and it didn't seem to me that my way of doing things was so very special. I felt I wasn't keeping up with the times. When this close friend of mine got married, I determined I was going to learn somehow to dance before the wedding."

She did, and she liked the experience. She kept on taking courses, each one built around some particular, and always rather simple, interest of hers. Then an accident occurred. "I was very interested in learning to play the recorder and signed up for the beginners' class. There were misprints in the catalogue and this class was on a different night and I couldn't make it. I had been thinking for a long time that I should take *Understanding Your Emotions* and I always kept putting it off for some time when it was more convenient, so when there was a mistake in the catalogue I decided that this was the time for me to take that course." With this decision, she confronted directly her own greatest need as, one suspects, she would not have been able to do earlier.

This illustration suggests that the original decision to learn needs to be reinforced by several other factors before one becomes a continuing learner: by a successful initial experience; by a variety of offerings at different levels of depth, so that the individual has the opportunity —even the enticement—to go on; and possibly by skillful and subtle guidance by teachers and counselors. The institution to which this young woman went may make an occasional mistake in its catalogue but it is outstanding for its quality, its variety of offerings, and its effort to provide individual assistance. "I had been thinking for a long time that I should take *Understanding Your*

Emotions"; perhaps this was a natural conclusion independently arrived at, but more likely it was the result of personal relations work handled with adroitness and finesse.

THE ACTIVITY-ORIENTED also begin their sustained participation in adult education at the point when their problems or their needs become sufficiently pressing. One man, now in his middle fifties, began to take part in group learning activities when he was in his late twenties, starting because he had no friends and was lonely; for almost thirty years now he has built a social life by taking courses and joining groups. The initiating power of a strong need is also seen in the lives of others: the young woman who realized in her mid-twenties that she would never be married if she did not take steps to put herself in the marriage market; the older woman who turned to education in her late forties because she needed to fill the void left by the marriage of her children and the death of her husband; and the man who saw that his chance to get ahead socially and professionally would be enhanced if he took a vigorous part in the educational activities of an organization to which some of the most distinguished citizens of his community belonged.

Some kind of self-recognition or personal stock-taking seems to occur among the activity-oriented (and perhaps among the other groups as well) before they take part extensively in educational pursuits. "You have to recognize that you're a person before you go and do anything about yourself" is the way one woman expressed this point, and, when invited to explain this unusual statement, she went on to say: "You don't develop any sense of discrimination until you have some frame of reference to discriminate about, some fore and after, right and left, or good and bad. You don't think about self-education unless you are aware of number one—you are a self, you are a person, you are somebody. Of course, people may be aware of themselves—that they have to eat when they're hungry and so on—but that they have anything beyond just physical characteristics I don't think they realize. You take all these people that you pass in the street, they are going around with blinders on and their eyes are almost completely shut. These people don't ever look at themselves as individuals; they just go on existing."

Perhaps the need for self-awareness is expressed most frequently and fluently by the activity-oriented because their needs are often so basic or so far-reaching. The man who has to keep on learning because his family has always been "forward-moving" is a man whose very integrity would be threatened if he failed to comply with his inherited code of values. His conception of himself is far more likely to be explicit and compelling than is that of the goal-oriented young woman whose idea of education is that it will enable her to dance at her friends' weddings.

A FEW LEARNING-ORIENTED individuals were also latecomers to adult education. One started at the age of twenty-seven and two others in their middle forties. But most of the learning-oriented follow a different pattern; they have been engrossed in learning as long as they can remember. Let us begin with the late-starters and then return to the others who commenced their careers of study much earlier.

The two who began in their early forties were keenly intelligent men who had been absorbed in practical affairs, were deeply engaged socially, and had built distinguished careers. Suddenly what they had was not enough. To the outsider, their lives would have seemed filled to the brim with the riches which come from success, from established position, and from a happy family and social life. But both of them found that they had margins of energy and attention, and all at once the pursuit of knowledge seemed challenging to them. The challenge has grown with their own accomplishments in learning. "I just decided one day I was bored," remarked one of them, "so I started looking around for things to do, and a brochure came in the mail that told about a course that looked interesting." And now he says: "I have one real big hell of an ambition. I just want to make enough money so that in about eight to ten years I can quit, while I'm still in my fifties. I'd like to go back to a university and really learn some of the things to which I was exposed in the courses there. I think the first thing I would want to do is probably to enroll full-time at some university."

The other man, older, more experienced, and more introspective, has long had the same ambition to study full-time, and is gradually achieving his wish, bringing his business career slowly to a close while he expands his learning activities. Yet fifteen years ago, when he took his first course, he did so impulsively, merely to accompany a friend. When asked why he thought he was a continuing learner, this man listed various factors: "Leisure time in sufficiency; dissatisfacton with my social environment; the opportunity presented in the field of education due to the fact that I live in Chicago." He had obviously thought carefully about the matter, possibly because he knew he was going to be interviewed; to a cross-checking question an hour or more later he answered that he carried on his study because of "sufficiency of means and leisure plus the opportunity."

While both of these men had completed college, they had regarded education as a necessary evil throughout their boyhoods and one of them had deliberately tried to get the lowest possible grades which would still permit him to be graduated. Nor had either of the men shown any interest in education in their earlier adulthood. Why they took up learning instead of golf, politics, or bridge remains a mystery.

As for the man who began his participation at the age of twenty-seven, his answer was simple and clear-cut. "The wife suggested I take some courses in English at night school," he answered and "influence of wife" might be duly noted if we could believe in single causes. But the interview itself unfolds a far more complex story of a boy who came of good stock and had a fine family relationship, even though his parents had little formal education; who, because his father developed tuberculosis, had to leave school at the end of the eighth grade and do what work he could find in the midst of the depression; who went away to a Civilian Conservation Corps camp and found new horizons there as well as an officer in the camp who served as a sympathetic and helpful counselor; who, on his return, got himself established in a skilled trade; who, when he was twenty-four, was driving the car when he had an unavoidable accident in which his best friend was killed; who found the parents of that friend so kind and so unreproaching that their attitude was a revelation to him; who became converted, as a result, to the religious faith of those parents; who was strongly influenced by a man at work who himself had a passion for learning; and, finally, whose wife suggested he take some courses in English at night school. It was a cataract of consequences or, as he put it himself, "A potential existed and a certain number of things had to happen to set this thing in motion." The result, whatever the combination of causes, is a truly learning-oriented man.

The pattern of these three persons seems consistent with that already found among the goal- and the activity-oriented. The rest of the learning-oriented, however, have been engrossed in learning as far back as their earliest memories take them and they present a more perplexing problem. The members of this particular group came to their interviews well equipped with answers and, as it turned out, these answers tended to be of two sorts.

The first was that the habit of learning stemmed from several causes. A good expression of this point of view came from the branch librarian: "The reasons why? I think my parents—I think that more than anything. Plus, well, of course, you need to be reasonably intelligent—that helps, too—and the good background of education —real, old-fashioned education with the emphasis on reading, writing, and arithmetic, which I think gives one a much better basis for enjoying education, and not just getting it, or pretending to get it." She had thought this matter through very carefully and, when it came up again an hour and a half later, she remarked, "Naturally after your letter I started thinking, 'Well, what does make me this sort of person?' It seemed to me that it was intelligence, family, and education, and really nothing else, but I might be oversimplifying it. There might be something else that I am not aware of—not very likely, though, because I'm quite introspective and I probably would discover something."

The second major viewpoint, expressed by some of the most sophisticated people interviewed, was that the habit of learning has nothing to do with environmental factors, but is associated in some manner with heredity. Several people seemed to believe this in their hearts but said so only obliquely, probably because they do not see how a habit can be inherited. But several persons spoke out clearly on the point. The most extreme position was put by one woman as follows: "I kind of go along with the idea of reincarnation. In the same family of, say, three children, you have one a very primitive kind of person, one a very mature, well-integrated kind of person, and one sort of in-between. It is almost as though the primitive person were starting out on this business of living, but the more mature person has been around several times and each time he has answered another problem or two and maybe he will finally get to the point that he'll answer the last couple of problems and then he won't have all this monkey business to go through again." When asked if she really believed this theory of hers, she answered, "I would say that I 51 per cent believe in it and 49 per cent don't believe in it."

The others who thought that the trait was hereditary

had come to this viewpoint simply because they could not conceive that any other explanation was possible. They had had seriously deprived childhoods and, looking back into the conditions of their lives from earliest infancy, they could find no trace of any positive influence in their environments. The desire to learn must therefore, as one man put it, have been caused by "a fortuitous union of chromosomes." His belief is worth developing a bit, partly because of who he is and partly because his views are expressed in one of the most eloquent passages to be found in all the interviews.

He is a Hoosier industrialist, now in his fifties, who lives in one of the regional cities which ring the state of Indiana. Partly because of his managerial and administrative skill and partly because of his distinguished career of public service, he is a man of means, of position, and of honor, known throughout his state. And yet he came from humble origins, his family spoke a foreign language, his mother died when he was an infant, and his father took little responsibility for him. He and his brothers and sisters were brought up as a collective responsibility by his relatives. But his very first Sunday School teacher later told him that, even before he could read and write, he was different from all the other children in his eagerness to learn. To this distinguished citizen, the reason he is a continuing learner appears clear:

I can't think of any better answer than to say that I was born with a good mind, an inquiring mind,[2] and that seems to be it. I'm not conscious of ever doing anything except what I was compelled and impelled to do. And many times, I was

[2] To him, though he must remain anonymous, I would like to express my thanks for giving me the title of this book.

almost helpless in the drift of it. I needed books, I needed knowledge, I needed information as much as I needed food, and it seemed as natural for me to go to the library. Now I'm not a bookish person as you can see. Nobody would say I'm a bookworm, that I'm monkish at all. I get along socially with people well; people like me, but there's just a deep core of something that's always been there with me. All I can say is "Thank God that it has." It's been a wonderful gift. I regard it as a gift. I can't say that it is something that I was without and realized its value and determined that I would acquire it; that is not so. There's always been that sponge-like thing inside of me that when I fed it a book or something it responded and that was it. I don't take any credit for it. I was born with it. I believe that. I was born with it.

Now, of course, there's the other possible answer which might be this, but I'm not convinced of it. Remember now I'm a boy that was born on the wrong side of the tracks. And I have my whole way to make and I'm unhappy in the way I live. I was unhappy at the way food was served at the table. Tell me why? I don't know why. Except I like to eat gracefully and I still do. I'm one of those men who will pay a lot of money for atmosphere in a restaurant. It has to have food, too! So that I was unhappy with the crudities, with the vulgarity, with the coarseness of my life. I don't know why. It'd been happier for me if I hadn't been. And so I determined early in life that I was going to get out of it. I bet I said that over to myself a thousand times a day. "I'm going to get out of it. I'm going to get out of it." Now how was I going to get out of it? I didn't have any money. I didn't have any social background. I found I had a brain that I could rely on. All right, so by doing good work and attracting people's attention, that was one of the ways I got out of it. Now maybe I started something like a cancer train with that tremendous determination but I don't think so, because even when none of these thoughts were present I would lie in a hammock in the back yard in the trees with a book and I couldn't go anywhere because we had no money, but I went to places that nobody went to. I went to Turkey and I went to India, and I always loved travel books, and I loved biographies of great men. I've always loved fine writing. I like fine, elegant, well-turned phrases and I've spent a great deal of time in polishing my language. I had the wish to learn. I didn't get it. I had it.

So MUCH FOR WHAT the continuing learners themselves say and believe, each one about himself. Now let us look at them as a whole, trying to discover what they have in common that might have led them to become continuing learners.

When this question is raised, one thinks at once of such factors as sex, age, nationality origin, religion, social status, and level of formal schooling, which are ordinarily so important as causes of behavior. The people studied here, however, were drawn from many of the segments of our society in order to concentrate on continuing learning itself. Because of the basic selection process, therefore, the influence of such factors as those named above cannot be measured, since no effort was made to construct a sample which would accurately reflect the total population. Nor is it possible in this study to examine the influence of such aspects of personality as intelligence, interest patterns, and temperament. These traits can be measured with greater or lesser accuracy but there is no comparable test to determine the extent to which people possess inquiring minds and consequently there is no way as yet to compare this trait with the others. Such tests are now in the making,[3] however, and

[3] Several investigators are now attempting to develop such a scale. Among them are Thomas Averill of Kansas State Uni-

it is hoped that their construction will be made easier by the present exploration in depth of a group of continuing learners.

Even when all of the foregoing factors are ruled out, however, a comparison of the case studies already collected permits a few observations about several of the influences which are most commonly suggested as leading to lifelong learning. They are family background, teachers and schools, public libraries, occupation, and the example of friends.

THE CONTINUING LEARNERS came from no single kind of home. Some had a warm family life, some a hateful one, and others none at all. Most of them had been brought up by both parents, some by only one, and some by neither. Some of the parents were continuing learners themselves and some were not. Some parents supported learning, some opposed it, and some were indifferent.

Nor is there a discernible difference among the three major groups except that, in the childhoods of the goal- and activity-oriented, one can often see developing the forces that led to education later. One mother, for example, wanted to keep her daughters with her always. As one of those daughters reported, "Our family was a self-satisfied, self-contained unit in itself. We did not need other people. We were our own entertainment. We sought each other's company much more than I think average, much more than was wise. We were raised to

versity; M. Alan Brown of the University of Colorado; Earl Hargett of the Northeast Mississippi Junior College; and Roy Ingham of Syracuse University.

do so many things on what was the QT. I wasn't supposed to let my Dad know when I got new shoes or anything. Everything was kept secret in the house, everything we wanted to do was done on the sly. My mother raised me to hate men." One needs no particular acuteness to see that this relationship would eventually create great needs when the daughters finally had to confront life, though it remains a mystery as to why, in this particular case, these needs were met constructively through education.

One factor which appears to be common to most of the people interviewed is the strength of their relationships to their parents. "Living with my family," observed one woman, "was like living with your nose against an electric light. It's nice to have a light but it's hard to be too close to it." There is no way of knowing, to be sure, whether this intensity of feeling is greater among continuing learners than among other people. But it could not be doubted that the strength of feeling, either for or against the parents, was present. "My mother, I might add here," said one woman, "has probably been the greatest inspiration for me doing all these things—because I just didn't want to be like my mother. I really think she was a terrific influence in that while I didn't know what I thought I'd be, I always said as a child I just didn't want to be like that." Another woman referred several times to her warm relationship with her father: "He used to sit up nights reading when I would be doing my arithmetic or something like that and I wasn't too good at arithmetic and sometimes I had to work very hard and late, and mother would tell me to come to bed but I would have to finish that job. Well, there would be my father reading—see, there he was for company, the two of us alone—that might have had something to do with it because my brothers and sisters didn't sit up and do that." The memory of those long evenings together is now fifty years old, but it is still vivid.

One learning-oriented man, who rejected education all his life until he was forty, had a powerful, though negative, relationship with his father. It was finally worked out in an illogical, though very human, way when the son adopted (on his own initiative, he insists) some of the very values against which he had rebelled when they were expressed by his father. The childhood antagonism was a general clash of two strong personalities, but its sorest point was the resentment of the boy against one demand made by the father. "He'd make it a point to be home at four o'clock in the afternoon and I was expected to meet him and spend an hour with him discussing or reading the Bible or some commentaries on the Bible. Even in the summers when the other kids were out playing, I had to be there at four o'clock, be on the porch so we could talk." This practice began when the boy was about eleven and it continued until he was about fifteen, when his antagonism grew so great that his father finally gave up. The end of the story comes in the ability of the son to tell this anecdote: "One day when my father came to visit me here and I had my own home and children, he and I were taking a walk. I said, 'You know, dad, I'm bringing up my children differently than you brought me up. I recall the austere principles you tried to put over with me and I don't think that's necessary. I think you were wrong in having those struggles with me when I was a boy.' And he said, 'Well, all

I can say in my defense is that I have an exhibit I'm willing to present. When you produce an exhibit as good as I have, then I will admit I may have been wrong.' "

THE STUDIES reviewed earlier show that the amount of formal schooling is more highly related to participation in educational activities than any other factor. This is not a simple cause-and-effect relationship. Schooling in childhood and education in adulthood are, in part at least, both products of such similar causes as the availability of educational opportunities, the influence of parents, and the ability of the students. Still, most people would readily agree that formal education is at least one of the causes of continuing learning because it helps in laying the groundwork for later study and in creating an awareness of the diversity of life and of knowledge.

It is surprising, therefore, that only one of the persons interviewed thought that teachers had had any influence in creating the desire to continue learning. Naturally everyone remembered his school days vividly and often had warm or antagonistic feelings toward certain teachers.[4] But when asked, perhaps rather insistently (for teaching is my own profession), whether teachers had been instrumental in creating the will to study or the habit of learning, the answer was almost always "no."

The explanation of this discordant finding may well

[4] When asked whether he remembered his teachers, one man gave me a quizzical look and said, "The Chicago schools are pretty peculiar places with very eccentric teachers. It would be pretty hard *not* to remember some of them." He was, of course, referring to the Chicago schools as they were many years ago.

be related to failures in the prevailing method of teaching. If a teacher does not make explicit the importance of lifelong learning, demonstrate its significance in his own behavior, and show by what methods it may be pursued, there is no particular reason why he should be identified by his students as wishing to create the desire for continuing education within them.

But this explanation is probably not sufficient. The deepening of the desire and capacity to learn involves the very quality of the teaching process itself. The master teacher makes every learning experience so inherently interesting and rewarding that curiosity is deepened, not dulled, and the desire to learn increases rather than diminishes. On this point, the observations of the one woman who felt that school was important in making her a continuing learner may be significant: "You never felt that you had to learn so many facts about so many things. It was more an exploration of the world of fact. It depended so much on the personality of the teachers and the personality of the principal. It wasn't that we didn't write examinations. We wrote far more than the children do now. And it wasn't because we didn't compete, because we did, we competed madly with each other. Yet we didn't feel bound in, hemmed in by facts; we weren't merely learning facts, we were learning. Learning for its own sake without any idea of getting on in the world or making more money or anything like that."

There is, of course, a less hopeful possibility, which is that teachers can do little or nothing to have themselves remembered as stimulators of continuing education. Perhaps it is their fate to have their students outgrow them so completely that no memory remains of a time when there was need and dependency. Perhaps the particular things one learns in school are like food; they nourish and build one up, but their details are as quickly forgotten as the menu of the dinner eaten a week ago last Thursday. Perhaps what is to be learned is itself so completely central that the teacher is merely the mediator. The devotees of Mozart, said Sacheverell Sitwell, "were won over, long ago, by some ravishment of the ears in a church, or they heard that incredible grace and delicacy in some concert-hall, or even on a gramophone." [5] But it is Mozart's music which matters and which is remembered, not the performers of his work.

The important consideration is not whether the teacher is remembered but whether the student becomes a continuing learner. Here it may be noted that all of the people interviewed belonged to a different generation from that which is now emerging from the schools. One of my colleagues, in making this point, observed that the amount of continuing learning is probably increasing because of the growing influence of progressive education. As he put it, "People who have been to a progressive school have the feeling that they don't know anything." Perhaps, though he meant to be cynical, he was really making a profound point; Socrates often announced that he didn't know anything either. But however we view the changes in the schools, let us remember that earlier eras have now presented us with their exhibits. When we are judged by the one we present, will we have done as well?

[5] *Mozart* (New York: D. Appleton and Company, 1932), pp. 1–2.

ALMOST ALL of the people who felt that they had been oriented toward learning since childhood mentioned the public library as a stimulating force in their development. Again and again the same story was repeated, but it was put most expressively by one man who, while talking generally about his childhood, suddenly broke through the surface flow of his memories to an old experience which obviously had great meaning and satisfaction for him: "When I was a kid in the third grade (and at that time we were very poor), I used to hitchhike to a place where there was a public library. I would spend my entire Saturdays there. I remember now (I haven't thought about this for years!) that library was just about one of the most wonderful places when I was a child. And there was a woman there, a librarian, who taught the story hour, who stimulated my interest a great deal in reading and she discovered that I was advanced in my reading and I guess I interested her for that reason."

Mr. James D. Meeks, the Director of the Dallas Public Library, recently asked each professional member of his staff to make a brief case study of a patron and has very kindly made the results available to me. The people described range widely in age but the total picture is one of imaginative and individualized assistance which must make the public library seem very close to the people of its community. Here for example is an account of a young man who, one may predict with some confidence, will become a learning-oriented adult:

At fifteen, Arthur's interests include photography, music, writing, religion, and psychology. A high school sophomore, he lives with his mother, grandmother, and brother. At the moment he is associated with Eagle Productions Movie

Company, a teenage group in which he has been writer, director, producer, and photographer. Being a little on the short side, Arthur is interested in getting some elevator shoes, but, like Dobie Gillis, his size does not keep him from having girl friends. He is in the band and orchestra at school and is a long-time member of the Creative Writing Club at the library. He writes short stories most of the time, has started a couple of novels, and turns out some pretty good poetry. Arthur comes to the library two or three times a week, using all of the departments except Family Living. His constant requests for suggestions on what to read keep us on our toes. New things are suggested as they come in, and older authors are recommended to fill in when new books are unavailable. (I wish I knew what to give him next!)

Arthur is probably having at least as vital an experience in school as in the Dallas Public Library but, if he proves to be like the adults studied here, he will, if interviewed in his forties, pay more tribute to the library than to the school. Why? We can only guess at the reasons. Perhaps his contact with the library is a freer one, more completely the result of his initiative, more individual, and less bound by necessary formal requirements. Perhaps the habit of reading is more readily transferred to adult life than the habit of course-taking. Perhaps the public library conveys the value of lifelong learning because it so obviously serves all age groups or because librarians consciously or unconsciously transmit this value.

COUNSELORS at adult educational institutions are often consulted by those who wish to escape from their present employment and seek to do so by means of education. Only two such persons were found in this study, perhaps because it did not include those whose primary participation was in diploma, degree, or certificate programs. Both of these persons disliked their present occupations, and their educational ventures were directed at least in part by a wish to escape, but, as it happened, neither had tangible goals in mind for their studies, and the desire for vocational change did not seem central to their purposes.

Among the others, one group was made up of those whose jobs did not seem to influence in any way the kind or amount of education they undertook. A second group was made up of those who have, as at least one of their motives, the desire to get ahead in their work. Sometimes this desire is straightforward, as it is with the man who is moving up the supervisory ladder and needs to know more and more about management. Sometimes the connection is not quite so obvious. "I don't think any good advertising man," said one of them, who, from outward appearances of success, was a very good one indeed, "can be so unless he has interests somewhere in the areas of the arts and philosophy. People in our business have to be creative in some way or other. Any area which requires the use of the mind offers you ideas that can be transferred. Take the most obvious thing: we are dealing with pictures in our business a great deal. Well, it goes without saying, then, that some understanding of art would be valuable. We're continuously attempting to develop people's opinions. Some knowledge of sociology and the way people think and what influences affect them, is important."

A third group is made up of people who have routine jobs, and who, partly to escape from them, have found

other avenues for their energy. Leadership in a union is
one such avenue which can absorb an endless amount of
time. ("You see," said one of the several union leaders
who were interviewed, "there are two types of people:
people who have a sense of mission in the union move-
ment and people who have families!") These avenues in
turn lead to education, which, while it is thus one step
removed from occupation itself, nonetheless arises indi-
rectly from it.

ONE KIND OF INFLUENCE which emerged clearly in the
interviews was that exerted by the continuing learners
themselves. Sometimes they merely have such a con-
tagious belief in the importance of education that they
infect those around them. Sometimes, however, they go
beyond unconscious influence to direct stimulation. Most
of the persons studied were either stimulators themselves
or had been stimulated by others. Some were both. One
of the men presented an excellent portrait of the stimulator at work:

When I was at the hospital a few years ago for some surgery,
I took Toynbee along with me. I had had it given to me as a
gift and it was something I wanted to get at. I started reading it and got into difficulty because my knowledge of the
geography and history of the ancient world was deficient.
So I talked to the visiting librarian who came around every
day and the head librarian came in to see me. She sent away
and got maps of the ancient world and they put them around
my room in the hospital and so I started reading Toynbee.
So pretty soon in came the doctor with his staff and said,
"What the hell have we got here?" "Well," I said, "I'm
reading Toynbee." "Oh, you are! I've been wanting to read

that, too. What's he say?" Well, he said so and so and so and so. Well, every day we finally developed a coffee hour in my room and pretty soon that circle broadened and changed and so forth and I had many top flight people from the clinic that came in there. What I was doing for them, I was going on and reading so that I could tell them what had happened since last time. It was a wonderful month. When we needed different maps the librarian got them. Some of the men bought Toynbee and started reading it.

Sometimes the influence of the stimulator lasts far longer than a month. During the first world war, a young intellectual moved into a small Illinois city to help carry on his family business. As soon as he was established, he formed what he called the Controversial Club and it has been meeting ever since. Its members, who are some of the leading men in the city, discuss many themes; among them have been the nature of the Renaissance, the writings of Virgil, how a scientist establishes his facts and conclusions, the logic which lies behind the law, the meaning of historical evidence, and the relationship among metaphysics, religion, and faith. While this example is outstanding in the range and depth of its interests, such clubs are by no means uncommon, judging by the experiences of the persons interviewed.

A stimulator is a crusader who uses personal influence. He has come to understand that continuing education can have great value as a method of achieving goals, as an activity in itself, or as a window opening on new vistas of knowledge. To this understanding, he often adds the fervor of a true believer and, in a rather surprisingly large number of cases, he seems convinced that he is the original discoverer of the value of lifelong education. To Tristram Shandy's father "It was a consuming vexation

. . . that my mother never asked the meaning of a thing she did not understand." [6] The stimulator is similarly vexed with the people about him. His missionary work has varying degrees of subtlety, ranging from the forthright ("I make people think and read whether they want to or not; I force them to do it") to the indirect ("I leave catalogues around in strategic spots").

The stimulator does not succeed in infecting everyone with his own zeal, for, like every other kind of message, his often falls on deaf ears. One stalwart old Wisconsin Progressive provides an example of what can happen. Although educated in a profession, he took a job as a semi-skilled laborer because he wanted to help working-class people learn how to better themselves. His activities were reported by one of the men he influenced: "We tried a discussion group. At the beginning the membership was rather high. But the interest, it waned. We rented a room downtown at a hotel. Met once a month. He put out a newsletter and in this newsletter he would put a few of his own ideas and ask for contributions. But the thing wasn't successful for unfortunately we didn't get enough of a nucleus to hold it together. We did struggle along for about two years. None of the other fellows followed any pattern of continuing interest in education so far as I know." When asked why this was true, the respondent answered, "I really don't know unless it would be that they are more satisfied than they think they are."

Still, this stimulator had made at least one convert, the man to whom I talked, and possibly many more. And the influence of other stimulators was evident throughout the

[6] Laurence Sterne, *Tristram Shandy* (New York: The Heritage Press, 1935), p. 322.

interviews, although it never appeared to be a sufficient cause by itself. The stimulator may be only a person who sets a match to a fire which is already laid—but to have fires, we must have matches.

THIS EFFORT TO EXPLORE the reasons why some people become continuing learners has made it clear that there is no simple answer to this complex question. At the end, as at the beginning, we realize that we must ask "whys?" not "why?" Probably we shall never get at all the facts, though further research should give much clearer answers. Each person is unique and his actions spring from a highly individualized and complex interaction of personal and social factors. One of the people interviewed perceived this fact very clearly. When asked why his sister, who grew up in almost precisely the same conditions he did, was not interested in learning, he responded, "I would say her intellectual achievements and her potential were not as great and while she is a nice person, by the very virtue of the fact of her potential not being so great, the things that happened to her couldn't have the same effect as the things that happened to me. No, apparently at first glance it is the same, but it is totally different. There is no similarity at all. She didn't react to the things that I do."

THE EMPHASIS on continuing learners throughout these lectures will not, I hope, be reminiscent of the ancient story about the cellist who played only one note, maintaining that it was the one for which all other cellists were restlessly seeking. But the single note sustained here is essential if we are ever to understand adult education and come to maturity in our practice in that field. And it is a note which has not yet been played very often.

The university is distinguished from the kindergarten chiefly by the difference in the maturity of the student, and adult education is distinguished in the same way from the schooling provided to children and youth. The study of the individual has been accepted as an important starting-point at the earlier levels of education. The theory and practice of adult education will not progress very far until they are based on an understanding of how mature people approach the tasks and opportunities of adulthood. The organized field of adult education is now fragmented into groups built around institutions, processes, and special approaches; it can gain coherence and unified strength only on the basis of common themes, one of the most significant of which is the nature of the adult learner.

We now see the value of widespread lifelong learning in professional and vocational accomplishment. The need to maintain and enhance occupational skills has been brought home forcefully by the competition of the market, the rapid advancement of knowledge in every field, the need to cope successfully with larger and more complex forms of organization both of men and of knowledge, and the steady raising of acceptable levels of performance. As a result, by specialized efforts in many fields, there have been great advances in in-service education. Every outstanding professional in any field today must regard himself as a learner, no matter how advanced his age.

By building a strong and coördinated national program of adult education, we might hope to broaden the spirit of inquiry, now manifest in special education for occupations, until it includes all aspects of personal and social life. While the desire and the ability to learn are not shared equally by everyone, both can be fostered by good teaching, by careful guidance, by building and enlarging sympathetic enclaves, and by providing a range of educational opportunities. These tasks are too great for partial and divided efforts. The inquiring minds of the past have produced most of the advances of civilization. Our hopes for the future must rest in large measure on our capacity to increase the number and the ability of those who continue all their lives to share in the benefits and the pleasures of intellectual inquiry.

A NOTE ON METHOD

THE INSTRUMENT USED in this study consists of two parts. The first is a two-page statement which introduces the idea of continuing education, describes the way in which the interview was to be conducted, and indicates the general nature of the questions which were to be asked. This first statement was sent in advance to anybody who agreed to be interviewed, and thereby served as a device to avoid or reduce tension, to diminish explanations at the interview itself, and to stimulate the respondents to think about the subject on which they were to be interviewed.

The second part of the instrument is a series of nineteen major questions with a number of sub-questions to be used when needed to probe or to amplify responses. These questions were designed to get at the following points: 1. Do continuing learners possess any particular characteristics which make them different from other people? 2. What were the factors that led them to become continuing learners? 3. What has been the history of their continuing education in the past? 4. How much education are they now undertaking and of what kinds? 5. How do they think society views continuing education? 6. How do they themselves view it?

Both parts of the instrument were examined for clarity and comprehensiveness by specialists in instrument construction and in adult education. Graduate seminars discussed the wording of every sentence in Part I and every question in Part II. Pre-tests were conducted to determine how well the instrument would stand the tests of practical application. These various processes led to many revisions, and several changes were also incorporated as a result of the first few interviews in the study itself.

Two of the persons interviewed were already known to me as a result of counseling and teaching activities. The remainder were secured by requesting the staff members of several adult educational agencies to suggest the names of people who fitted clearly within the category of those whom I wanted to interview. Each such person was then asked by some staff member whom he knew to participate in this study. If a favorable response was secured, Part I of the instrument was sent to the potential interviewee and a time for the interview was set. An effort was made to secure as diverse a group of cases as possible, although no formal sampling procedure was used. For example, it was originally planned to have an equal number of men and women; as it turned out, there were 12 men and 10 women. Since nobody can be certain how continuing learners, as a group, are divided between the two sexes, there did not appear to be any way to establish a sample which would conform in this respect, or in any other, to the unknown dimensions of the total population.

So far as age was concerned, 2 of the people interviewed were under 35, 10 were from 35 to 50, 8 were from 50 to 65, and 2 were over 65. Twelve were married, 1 was divorced, and 9 were single. One was estimated to be in the upper class, 5 in the upper middle class, 13 in the lower middle class, and 3 in the lower class. Twenty-one were white and 1 was non-white. Eighteen were native-born and 4 foreign-born. In terms of highest level of formal education achieved, 2 had had less than an eighth-grade education, 2 had had some high school, 1 was a high school graduate, 5 had had some college work, 10 were college graduates, and 2 had pursued advanced studies.

The persons interviewed all lived within a radius of seventy-five miles of Chicago and all but two of the interviews were conducted in that city. Various offices and conference rooms were used to suit the convenience of the person interviewed. In every case, the physical setting was one in which quiet conversation could take place and all interruptions could be avoided. The recording equipment was operated in an adjacent room so as not to be an intrusion. The average interview took slightly longer than two hours, though the range was from forty-five minutes to three and one-half hours.

The social setting was as relaxed as possible. A preliminary conversation was held to establish rapport and to answer any questions which the person to be interviewed might have. When he seemed ready to proceed, the microphone was plugged in and the interview began. The interview was as unstructured as possible; the subject was encouraged to talk freely and discursively. The interviewer merely saw to it that sometime during the interview all of the questions on the instrument were dealt with.

When the interview drew naturally to a close, the

microphone was disconnected. A short informal conversation then took place dealing with such matters as the expression of thanks for the time given by the subject or a discussion of the weather. Just before the subject prepared to leave, he was asked whether the microphone had troubled him, whether he had any questions to ask now that it was turned off, and whether he had thought of anything he would like to add to the interview. These latter questions were designed not only to secure additional information but also to discover whether the recording process had led to any tension or repression of information. Almost nothing new was added at this point and the presence of the microphone did not appear to have had any significant effect.

When the person interviewed had taken his departure, the interviewer re-connected the microphone and dictated into it a description of him, any facts which had come to light in the post-recording session, and any thoughts or conclusions to which the interviewer had come as a result of the interview.

An effort was made to keep each interview separate from the others, so that attention could be focussed upon each individual. The effort to make any comparisons was resisted. The tapes of the first interviews were played back and discussed with several competent interviewers in order to eliminate errors of method, but subsequently there was no return to an interview in either taped or transcribed form until all of them had been completed.

At that point, all cases were read and the major themes for analysis were identified. The nature of these themes may be indicated by citing a few of them: home influences in childhood; present educational activities; the in-

fluence of libraries and reading; how the person interviewed believes he is viewed by society; and the factors
which he believes led him to become a continuing learner.
Broadly speaking these themes corresponded to the questions asked on the interview schedule, although some
questions could be combined into a single theme and
others proved generally unproductive and were elimi-
nated. Other themes—such as the significance of stimulators and of enclaves—emerged during the course of
reading through the cases.

Each case was then analyzed, the relevant items concerning each theme being copied from wherever they
might appear throughout the interview. Direct quotation
rather than summarization was used in order to keep the
flavor of the original material. Thus the analysis of Case
D in terms of the theme "Enclaves" has three quotations
drawn from widely separated parts of the transcript of
that case. If a given quotation had relevance to several
themes, it was included in each.

During this process, it became apparent that the people studied, while basically similar, fell into certain significant groups. Various categorizations were tried and
gradually modified until the present three-part classification (goal-, activity-, and learning-oriented continuing
learners) finally emerged and was clarified by further
analysis and application to the cases themselves.

Finally the various themes were studied both independently and in terms of the basic three-part classification.